# Social Change
# and the Electoral Process

William L. Shade

University of Florida Press / Gainesville / 1973

## EDITORIAL COMMITTEE

*Social Sciences Monographs*

Library of Congress Cataloging in Publication Data

Shade, William L.      1945–
  Social change and the electoral process.

  (University of Florida social sciences monograph
no. 49)
  Includes bibliographical references.
  1. Presidents—United States—Election—History.
2. United States—Social conditions.  I. Title.
II. Series:  Florida.  University, Gainesville.
University of Florida monographs.  Social sciences
no. 49.
JK524.S5        329′.023′7309        73–7713
ISBN 0–8130–0390–3

For
Billy, Elizabeth, Michael,
and their Mother

# Preface

$M$ORE THAN a decade ago the late E. E. Schattschneider, in *The Semi-Sovereign People*, put forth a serious challenge to students of the American political process: "The great problem in American politics is: What makes things happen? We might understand the dynamics of American politics if we knew what is going on when things are happening. What is the process of change? What does change look like?" This work is an attempt to deal with Schatt-schneider's challenge by answering the question "What is going on when things are happening in the American political system?"

First we require a definition of what "things are happening" in American politics, and this is undertaken in chapters one through four. The first is an integrative review of theories of American political development and voting behavior, and I present two contradictory portraits of the "things that happened" in American political history. Chapter two contains an alternative theory of political development to try to reconcile the contradictions in chapter one. In chapters three and four I examine the alternative theory in light of an empirical view of the American electoral process, classifying each presidential election from 1860 to 1968 according to "what happened" within the electorate. The election types are the "things that happened" in American political history.

In chapter five I look at the "what is going on" part of Schatt-schneider's query by identifying and interpreting trends in social, political, economic, intellectual, and technological change, shifts that are associated with particular electoral outcomes. The final chapter is a critical evaluation of the earlier theory in light of the empirical findings in chapter five.

I gratefully acknowledge the influence and direction of Frank J. Munger, who supervised the development of this work as my dissertation. I would also like to give credit to several former professors, particularly Manning J. Dauer, Richard L. Sutton, and David T. Hughes, and many fellow students, especially Richard Dodson and John Korey. While I deeply appreciate the contributions of these individuals, they should suffer no embarassment for any failings resulting from my misapplication of their wisdom.

WILLIAM L. SHADE

*Southern Illinois University*

# Contents

# 1. Theories of American Social Development

For more than twenty years political science has been involved in a crisis of epistemology. The discipline has split into two camps that have come to be known as "traditionalists" and "behavioralists." While there are many differences, a clear point of dichotomy has been the selection of research techniques.[1] Traditionalists tend to employ popular forms of historical analysis, e.g., vicarious participant observation, and to chronicle their findings after application of their individually developed standards of reason. Behavioralists tend to abhor the "subjectivity" of the traditional approach, and prefer more structurally developed standards of verification, such as mathematical statistics. I will now examine and compare theories of American history and American politics developed by both schools, and note their degree of theoretical overlap despite their differences in method of development.

## IDEOLOGICAL CONSENSUS
## AND ENVIRONMENTAL DETERMINISM

One area of overlap appears between traditional theories of an ideological consensus in American history and behavioral theories of environmentally determined voting behavior.

*Traditional Theories of Ideological Consensus.*—A main tenet of the "consensus" school of historians and traditional political scientists is that American political history is best explained in terms of

1. For examples of both the breadth of the split and its historical longevity, see the following: Gabriel Almond, Lewis Dexter, William Whyte, and John Hamilton Hallowell, "Politics and Ethics: A Symposium," *American Political Science Review* 40 (1946): 283–312; David G. Smith, David Apter, and Arnold Rogow, "A Symposium," *American Political Science Review* 51 (1957): 734–75; Heinz Eulau, *The Behavioral Persuasion in Politics* (New York: Random House, 1963); and Christian Bay, "Politics and Pseudopolitics," *American Political Science Review* 59 (1965): 39–51.

a common ideological consensus that has maintained the integrity and continuity of the American political community for nearly two hundred years. These theorists argue that those who focus their attention on internal political conflict ignore the boundaries of that conflict laid out by the "basic American consensus." This primary tenet has been succinctly stated by Richard Hofstadter: "Societies [like the United States] have a kind of mute organic consistency. They do not foster ideas that are hostile to their fundamental working arrangements. Such ideas may appear, but they are slowly and persistently insulated. . . . They are confined to small groups of dissenters and alienated intellectuals, and except in revolutionary times they do not circulate among practical politicians. The range of ideas, therefore, which practical politicians can conveniently believe in, is normally limited by the climate of opinion that sustains their culture."[2] But while consensus theorists agree on this basic point, they offer a wide variety of opinion as to the actual content of the basic consensus.

Hofstadter finds longitudinal ideological consistency based on economic beliefs: "The fierceness of the political struggles has often been misleading, for the range of vision embraced by the primary contestants in the major parties has always been bounded by the horizons of property and free enterprise. However much at odds on specific issues, the major political traditions [of the parties] have shared a belief in the rights of property, the philosophy of economic individualism, the value of competition; they have accepted the economic virtues of capitalist culture as necessary qualities of man" (p. viii). Thus, for Hofstadter, the primacy of the capitalist ideal has been the sustaining force in American history.

Louis Hartz relates the cohesiveness of the American community to two factors of its early developmental period, the absence of feudalism to kindle a revolutionary tradition (in the sense of the French Revolution) and the early importation and dominance of the philosophical ideals of John Locke.[3] For Hartz, the American tradition, or ideology, consists of the Lockean conception of the natural rights of man to life, liberty, and (as amended by Jefferson) the pursuit of happiness. The absence of feudalism permitted these ideals to spread and to take hold in the new nation,

2. *The American Political Tradition* (New York: Knopf, 1948), pp. viii–ix.
3. *The Liberal Tradition in America* (New York: Harcourt, Brace, 1955), chap. 1.

unchallenged by remnants of philosophies of divine right. The liberal tradition that developed, Hartz argues, has provided the fiber that has bound the nation together through its history. Thus Hartz' conception of the basic American consensus differs somewhat from Hofstadter's.

Daniel Boorstin has proposed that the American consensus is basically an antiphilosophy: "an unspoken assumption, an axiom, so basic to our thinking that we have hardly been aware of it at all. This is the axiom that institutions are not and should not be the grand creations of men toward large ends and outspoken values; rather they are organisms which grow out of the soil in which they are rooted and out of the tradition from which they have sprung. . . . We have become the exemplars of the continuity of history. . . ."[4] The American tradition for Boorstin lies in a national sense of "giveness," a self-conceptualized destiny that adapts itself to the circumstances of its age. He veers close to an environmentalist view of history, as he indicates: "If we have learned anything from our history it is . . . the value of both environmentalism and traditionalism as principles of political life, as ways of saving ourselves from the imbecilities, the vagaries and the cosmic enthusiasms of individual men" (pp. 185–86). Thus he argues that what has held the nation together is not a set of defined political ideals but rather an adaptability to environment. The strength of the American nation evolved as this adaptability was tested in the opening of geographical frontiers. Boorstin sees the American consensus not as a set of values, but as a historical fact of life. Indeed he argues that it would be futile to try to export an American philosophy, for none exists as an exportable commodity. America, for Boorstin, is a historical accident.

While offering divergent opinions on the content of the American consensus, the consensus theorists agree fundamentally that some form of ideological (or anti-ideological) consistency has dominated our political history. There are traditionalists who contradict the consensus school of history, and they will be considered later. *Behavioral Theories of Environmental Determinism.*—Behaviorally oriented scholars have long considered the rationale behind individual voting decisions. One school argues that the voting decision

4. *The Genius of American Politics* (Chicago: University of Chicago Press, 1953), p. 6.

is primarily a subconscious act, determined by the individual's environment at some time in the present or past. The precise environment is not agreed upon, and at least three theories of environmental determinism have been proposed.

The first appeared in Paul F. Lazarsfeld, Bernard R. Berelson, and Hazel Gaudet's *The People's Choice*,[5] an analysis of voting behavior in an Ohio county during the 1940 presidential campaign. In this work, and in its sequel, *Voting*,[6] an analysis of the 1948 voting decisions of 1,000 citizens of Elmira, New York, Lazarsfeld and his associates argued that the voting decision reflected primarily three factors of the individual's immediate environment, his socioeconomic status, his religion, and his place of residence (urban-rural). Ideological conflict was not apparent to any significant extent.

The Lazarsfeld studies, based at Columbia University, were followed by two studies from the University of Michigan Survey Research Center (SRC). In *The Voter Decides* and *The American Voter*,[7] the authors analyzed the comparative impact of party identification, candidate orientation, and issue orientation on the voting decisions of a nationwide sample of citizens in the elections of 1948, 1952, and 1956. Results showed that an enduring party identification, formed early in life and generally in a family environment, was the greatest single determinant of the voting decision. Like the Lazarsfeld studies, Campbell and his associates argued that the electorate paid little attention to issues or ideological differences between parties: "In general, people pay much less attention to political events and issues than is commonly realized. . . . Many people fail to appreciate that an issue exists, others are insufficiently involved to pay attention to recognized issues, and still others fail to make connections between issue positions and party policy."[8] The Michigan analysts argued that the environment with the greatest effect on the individual voter was not his immediate surroundings, as Lazarsfeld suggested, but rather his childhood and early adulthood, in which he was "politicized"

5. New York: Columbia University Press, 1948.
6. Berelson, Lazarsfeld, and William N. McPhee, *Voting* (Chicago: University of Chicago Press, 1954).
7. Angus Campbell, Gerald Gurin, and Warren E. Miller, *The Voter Decides* (Evanston: Row, Peterson, 1954); Campbell, Phillip E. Converse, Miller, and Donald E. Stokes, *The American Voter* (New York: Wiley, 1960).
8. *The American Voter*, pp. 182–83.

to one party or another. In essence, the Michigan analysts substituted a social psychological determinism for the Columbia analysts' sociological determinism.

Psychiatrist Richard E. Renneker analyzed clinical reports on neurotic patients undergoing psychoanalysis during the 1948, 1952, and 1956 elections and compared the data with information on their voting decisions. He concluded that the presidential candidate is commonly seen by the subconscious as a father substitute and that "father identification" was a critical subconscious determinant of candidate choice.[9]

These three theories of voting behavior differ on the precise environmental factors involved, but concur in the argument that the voting decision is primarily a subconscious act. There is congruence of these theories and the traditional ideological consensus theories.

*Ideological Consensus and Environmental Determinism: Theoretical Overlap.*—The relationship of the ideological consensus theories to environmental determinism was alluded to by Boorstin. If a political community is dominated by a single ideology throughout its history, political conflict must take root in some other form of social or psychological cleavage. The authors of *Voting* clearly subscribed to a consensus theory of political history, for they concluded their volume with a quote from Cobban: "For a century and a half the Western democracies have been living on the stock of basic political ideas that were last restated toward the end of the eighteenth century" (p. 323). Thus these divergent theories of American history and politics, developed by schools of diverse epistemological standards and methods, are found to be interdependent. The ideological consensus theory requires a phenomenon to account for political conflict, and environmental determinism provides it. Environmental determinism, congruently, denies the existence of widespread ideological conflict, and the existence of a historically dominant ideology (or anti-ideology) accounts for the lack of conscious interest in issues by the electorate. These two sets of theories present a unified view of American history and politics as ideologically dormant, a view, however, contradicted by competing elements within both schools.

9. "Some Psychodynamic Aspects of Voting Behavior," in *American Voting Behavior*, eds. Eugene Burdick and Arthur J. Brodbeck (New York: Free Press, 1959), p. 404.

### IDEOLOGICAL CONFLICT
### AND RATIONAL ACTION

Another area of theoretical overlap between the traditional and behavioral schools of political science arises from a consideration of traditional theories of historical ideological conflict and behavioral theories of rational action in voting behavior.

*Traditional Theories of Historical Ideological Conflict.*—The traditionalist school's view of historical ideological conflict counters consensus theorists' argument that American history is dominated by a commitment to a single ideology. In general, the conflict theorists argue that American political history has been characterized by two competing ideologies, one based on Enlightenment humanitarianism and the other on British laissez-faire. This argument, first made explicit by Vernon Louis Parrington, in his classic *Main Currents in American Thought*,[10] has developed into a theory that views American history as a series of sequences in which one of these competing ideologies dominated political life. Parrington, analyzing the period 1790–1920, named three successive periods in which one of these philosophies held sway: Jeffersonian humanitarianism, 1790–1828; Jacksonian individualism, to the end of the nineteenth century; a return to humanism with Progressivism, dominant until the election of Harding in 1920.

Merle Curti, another conflict theorist, looked for periods of ideological transition in the 1800–1950 span, and identified five eras in which he argued that a single ideology dominated: 1800–1830, patrician ideals; 1830–50, egalitarianism; 1850–70, triumphant nationalism; 1870–1900, corporate individualism; and 1900–1950, diversion, criticism, and contraction dominated by widespread pessimism and uncertainty, with no positive ideological theme.[11] More recently, Theodore Lowi cut a broader swath and outlined three dominant "public philosophies": 1776–1890, laissez-faire capitalism; 1890–1932, conflict between capitalism and pluralism; 1932–67, interest-group liberalism.[12]

These three conflict theorists obviously do not concur, except in very broad outline, on what philosophies dominated what period of American history, just as the consensus theorists did not agree

10. New York: Harcourt Brace, 1930.
11. *The Growth of American Thought*, 2d ed. (New York: Harper, 1951).
12. *The End of Liberalism* (New York: Norton, 1969).

on the precise content of consensus. The conflict theorists do share the belief that, as the United States developed, there has been competition between systems of philosophical political beliefs, and that within periods of the dominance of a single ideology, politics adheres to the tenets of that system rather than to one which dominated in another period of American history. In order to sustain such a theory of history there must be found in the community some mechanism for the transfer of belief systems, and this is the point at which the traditional theory of ideological conflict can be seen to overlap with behavioral theories of rational action.

*Behavioral Theories of Rational Action.*—Just as traditionalist scholars disagreed on the role of ideology in American history, behavioral scholars disagree on its role in the individual voting decision. The "rational actor" theory of voting behavior challenges the theories of the environmental determinists.

Rational actor theorists see the voter comparing the stands of the parties and candidates with his personal ideology and, on that basis, making a conscious choice. Perhaps the foremost proponent of this theory in political science was the late V. O. Key, Jr. He and Frank Munger were among the first to criticize the social determinism of the Lazarsfeld studies. In an analysis of historical voting patterns in Indiana, they concluded, "Yet there seems to be always a very considerable part of the electorate for which no readily isolable social characteristic 'explains' political preference. The query may be raised whether a rather serious void does not exist in the [social determinist] theory."[13]

Another critic of the environmental determinists attacked their method of finding the issue orientations of the electorate. In rather straightforward terms, E. E. Schattschneider counseled, "One implication of public opinion studies ought to be resisted . . . the implication that democracy is a failure because the people are too ignorant to answer intelligently all the questions asked by the pollsters. This is a professorial invention for imposing professorial standards on the political system, and deserves to be treated with extreme suspicion. Only a pedagogue would suppose that the people must pass some kind of an examination to qualify for participation in democracy. Who, after all, are these self-appointed censors who

---

13. "Social Determinism and Electoral Decision," in Burdick and Brodbeck, p. 298.

assume that they are in a position to flunk the whole human race?"[14]

Beginning in the mid–1960s with publication of Key's *The Responsible Electorate*,[15] a new body of literature has developed to support the rational action thesis of voting behavior. Key presented this thesis succinctly: "The perverse and unorthodox argument . . . is that voters are not fools. To be sure, many individual voters act in odd ways indeed; yet in the large the electorate behaves about as rationally and responsibly as we should expect, given the clarity of the alternatives presented to it and the character of the information available to it" (p. 7). Using survey data from the Gallup and Roper polls since 1936, Key analyzed the relationship of individual voting decisions to opinions on issues, and concluded, "In American presidential campaigns of recent decades the portrait of the American electorate that develops from the data is not one of an electorate straight-jacketed by social determinants or moved by subconscious urges. . . . It is rather one of an electorate moved by concern about central and relevant questions of public policy, of governmental performance, and of executive personality" (pp. 7–8).

Findings similar to Key's have begun to appear regularly in professional journals and at professional meetings. An extensive analysis of voting behavior in the 1968 presidential election was carried out by the University of North Carolina Comparative State Elections Project. Complete results will be published in a monograph; preliminary findings tend to provide support for the rationality of the individual voter. The analysts considered the voter's perceived proximity to each of the candidates in terms of issues, party, liberalism-conservatism, and social status. Using statistical causal modeling techniques to control for spurious relationships, they found issue proximity to be the most effective indicator of the vote where conditions permitted issues to be used. The preliminary report concluded with "If our preliminary findings do not transform our picture of the American voter from that of the automaton . . . to that of the rational hero of the civics books, we think that they certainly suggest that issues can and did 'count,' and that not a few of those who voted in November, 1968 were

14. *The Semi-Sovereign People* (New York: Holt, Rinehart, and Winston, 1960), p. 135.
15. Cambridge: Harvard University Press, 1966.

behaving rationally or, more likely, that many of them were behaving with more than a modicum of rationality."[16]

Secondary analysis of Survey Research Center data by David E. Repass contradicted the deterministic findings developed from those same data by the SRC analysts.[17] He searched open-ended interview material for clues to determine which issues were salient to individual voters, thereby avoiding the "professorial fallacy" alluded to by Schattschneider. Repass found, in the SRC survey for the 1964 election, that large numbers of voters accurately perceived party differences on issues that were salient to them, and cast their votes accordingly, thus raising the question of how sensitive conclusions based on survey research are to the types of questions employed in the analysis.

Other recent research supporting the rational voter theory could be described,[18] but the research presented seems sufficient documentation that a school of behavioralism has developed that challenges the environmentalist findings.

*Ideological Conflict and Rational Action: Theoretical Overlap.—* The theories of ideological consensus and environmental determinism were shown to be mutually dependent; a similar relationship exists between theories of ideological conflict and rational action, and this relationship was recognized by a proponent of one of the theories involved. Key saw that if issues and ideology were found to be evident in determining individual voting decisions, then the aggregated decisions must contain elements of issue-oriented or ideological conflict. He attacked those who put forth the consensus theory of American history: "The concept of consensus serves as a handy crutch for those who seek to explain . . . the American political system. . . . The magic word 'consensus' in short solves many puzzles, but only infrequently is the term given precise

16. David M. Kovenock, Phillip L. Beardsley, and James W. Prothro, "Status, Party, Ideology, Issues, and Candidate Choice: A Preliminary, Theory Relevant Analysis of the 1968 American Presidential Election," presented at the Eighth World Congress of the International Political Science Association, Munich, Germany, August 31–September 5, 1970, p. 22.

17. "Issue Salience and Party Choice," *American Political Science Review* 65 (1971): 389–400.

18. For other examples of research demonstrating the partial rationality of the voter see Gerald Kramer, "Short-Term Fluctuations in U.S. Voting Behavior, 1896–1964," *American Political Science Review* 65 (1971): 131–43, and Herbert F. Weisberg and Jerrold G. Rusk, "Dimensions of Candidate Evaluation," *American Political Science Review* 64 (1970): 1167–85.

meaning. Even less often are inquiries made about the distribution among the population of whatever attitudes, beliefs, or behaviors constitute consensus."[19]

The mutual dependence of the theories of ideological and rational action is readily discerned. If there are ideological changes in the theory of government, some mechanism in society must be responsible for effecting the change. The voting mechanism can fulfill that function if the individual voter is found to base his decision on consideration of issues. If he does, ideological conflict would be expected to occur at the aggregated, or national, level. The coalescence of these two theories then provides a second view of American history and politics that contradicts the view presented by analyzing the integration of the theories of ideological consensus and environmental determinism.

Thus the student appears to be faced with two contradictory interpretations of American history, one stressing its consensual development, the other emphasizing its philosophical conflicts. An alternative theory of American political development will now be proposed, and I will argue that it is capable of integrating and assimilating many of the theoretical differences between these two views of American history.

19. *Public Opinion and American Democracy* (New York: Knopf, 1961), p. 27.

# 2. The Theory of Political Paradigms

In HIS modern classic *The Structure of Scientific Revolutions,* Thomas S. Kuhn presented a theory of how science has remained continuous while espousing contradictory belief systems at various times.[1] His basic argument is that there are historical periods of "normal science" in which a certain belief system, or paradigm, dominates scientific investigation. Scientists are not value-free, but rather value-biased toward the principles which comprise the paradigm. Scientific revolutions occur with the rise of a new paradigm which can explain phenomena considered anomalous to the preceding paradigm; it then attracts an enduring group of adherents from competing modes of scientific activity. With the completion of this transformation, in which conflict among scientists is likened by Kuhn to conflict in political revolutions, the scientific enterprise returns to a stable condition of normal science, although functioning under the beliefs and principles of the newly adopted paradigm.

As an example, Kuhn notes that during the eighteenth century scientific investigation in physics proceeded under the assumption that light was material corpuscles, as described in Newton's *Opticks.* In the early nineteenth century, Young and Fresnel found that consideration of light as transverse wave motion provided a better explanation of observed physical phenomena, and the Young-Fresnel optical paradigm was adopted in place of the Newtonian concept. In this century, Einstein, Planck, and others proposed that additional explanatory power could be obtained by rejecting the Young-Fresnel paradigm and considering light as photons, i.e., quantum-mechanical entities with some characteristics of waves and some of particles.[2] Current physical research and

1. Chicago: University of Chicago Press, 1962 (2d ed. 1970).
2. For a more complete discussion of the shifts in physical paradigms, see Kuhn, pp. 11–13.

11

physics textbooks proceed under this assumption. Thus, science has maintained continuity of development while proceeding at various times under contradictory conceptions of a basic physical phenomenon. While this is an example of one small field of science, Kuhn shows that similar transformations have occurred elsewhere.

Kuhn's book is considered a classic work in the history of science, but few see it as Kuhn described it in his introduction, as an analysis of the intellectual behavior of members of a community. In the postscript to the second edition, Kuhn acknowledges the generalizability of the concept to other fields: "Having opened this postscript by emphasizing the need to study the community structure of science, I shall close by underscoring the need for similar and, above all, for comparative study of the corresponding communities in other fields. How does one elect and how is one elected to membership in a particular community, scientific or not? What is the process and what are the stages of socialization to the group? What does the group collectively see as its goals; what deviations, individual or collective, will it tolerate; and how does it control the impermissible abberation?" (p. 209). I will attempt to extend Kuhn's theory of intellectual behavior to the American political community, and to postulate a theory of political paradigms.

As Kuhn uses it, the term paradigm has two senses. In one, it is used to describe the content of belief systems shared by members of a community. Kuhn refers to this use as the sociological definition of the term, that is, a synonym for sociological phrases such as "normative consensus." In its second use, the word refers to an explicit exemplary past achievement, a single element of the shared belief system, in Kuhn's words, "one sort of element in that constellation [of beliefs], the concrete puzzle-solutions which, employed as models or examples, can replace explicit rules as a basis for the solution of the remaining puzzles of normal science" (p. 175).

Generalization of the first meaning to the political community is readily accomplished, for no community exists without some organizing principle or ideology, and to apply the term paradigm to the content of specific organizing principles at a point in time is simply a question of selection of nomenclature.

The second sense of the word, the puzzle-solving, exemplary

past achievement, requires a more detailed look at the dynamics of change in the political community. Political ideologies, unlike scientific paradigms, are rarely, if ever, "discovered." They develop over time, and the transformation of ideological tenets into specific policies for the political community consumes even more time. However, political scientists have demonstrated single points in history at which sharp and drastic shifts in the conduct of government of the American political community have been effected. The reference is to the phenomenon of "critical elections," first developed by Key in 1955.[3]

In his original conception, Key described critical elections as "a category of elections in which voters are, at least from impressionistic evidence, unusually deeply concerned, in which the extent of electoral involvement is relatively quite high, and in which the decisive results of the voting reveal a sharp alteration of the preexisting cleavage within the electorate [which] seems to persist for several succeeding elections" (p. 4). Thus, these elections have characteristics analogous to those of paradigm-shifting scientific discoveries. Kuhn's two conditions necessary for a paradigm shift are the capacity of the contending paradigm to do two things: to attract adherents from the previously dominant paradigm, and to propose solutions to unsolved problems facing the community (p. 10). Critical elections clearly perform the first function: a sharp and drastic shift in party loyalties occurs, and it endures for several succeeding elections. But fulfillment of the second condition requires that critical elections be accompanied by ideological conflict, and that the electorate select a new ideological paradigm that it felt offered more "concrete puzzle-solutions" than the existing ideological framework.

Research built upon Key's original thesis has suggested the existence of such conflict. An up-to-date summary was recently provided by Walter Dean Burnham: "To recapitulate, then, eras of critical realignment are marked by short, sharp reorganizations of the mass coalitional bases of the major parties which occur at periodic intervals on the national level; are often preceded by major third party revolts which reveal the incapacity of 'politics as usual' to integrate, much less aggregate, emergent political demand; are closely associated with abnormal stress in the socio-

3. "A Theory of Critical Elections," *Journal of Politics* 17 (1955): 1–18.

economic system; are marked by ideological polarizations and issue-distances between the major parties which are exceptionally large by normal standards; and have durable consequences as constituent acts which determine the outer boundaries of policy in general, though not necessarily of politics in detail."[4] Burnham's indication of the ideological intensity of critical elections tends to support the conclusion that the electorate is responding to an offer of more concrete puzzle-solutions to the concomitant "abnormal stress" in the social system. Thus, critical elections seem to fulfill the second condition for a paradigm shift, i.e., of exemplary past achievement (in this case an achievement of party and candidate rather than of scientists) which "can replace explicit rules as a basis for the solution of the remaining puzzles" of normal politics (rather than science).

The analogy of political paradigms is now complete. To paraphrase the description of scientific paradigms, there are historical periods of normal politics in which a certain belief system, or paradigm, dominates political activity. Politicians are not ideology-free, but rather ideology-biased toward the principles which comprise the paradigm. Political paradigm shifts occur when a new paradigm arises which, in the judgment of the electorate, better accounts for phenomena which were considered anomalous to the preceding paradigm, and which succeeds in attracting adherents (voters) away from competing modes of political activity. This process culminates at a critical election; when it is completed, the political community then returns to a stable condition of normal politics, though now functioning under the beliefs and principles of the newly adopted paradigm.

Application of the theory of political paradigms to American history can reduce the wide theoretical gap between the traditionalist schools of ideological conflict and ideological consensus. Each of the competing traditionalist schools can be said to have identified a separate aspect of the process of paradigm formulation. The consensus theorists note the two-century continuity of the community, while the conflict theorists point to several shifts in the content of political paradigms throughout that period. Within the theory of political paradigms, the seemingly contradictory conclusions of the two schools are reduced to a difference in emphasis,

4. *Critical Elections and the Mainsprings of American Politics* (New York: Norton, 1970), p. 10.

for the theory holds that the community can effect a shift in paradigm content without a loss of continuity. And, while paradigm shifts point to ideological conflict, the theory does not preclude the existence of a long-run common ideological thread within the paradigm, such as a commitment to the intrinsic freedom of man (similar to the long-run commitment of the scientific community to the principle of objective verification). Commitment to individual freedom, however, could prescribe one set of policies under one paradigm, and a seemingly contradictory set under another. Thus, while both Herbert Hoover and Richard Nixon have proclaimed themselves advocates of free economic competition, Nixon's proposed national health program would look scandalously socialistic to Hoover but is currently branded conservative by Edward Kennedy. Nixon is the economic conservative within the current paradigm, or "rules of the game," and intra-paradigm conflict must be distinguished from paradigm-shifting conflict. Intra-paradigm conflict revolves around interpretation of how paradigm content is to be translated into public policy, not around the content of the paradigm itself. It is this characteristic that distinguishes periods of normal politics from periods of paradigm shifts, and this is a point that has been obscured in the arguments of the traditionalist scholars of the conflict and consensus schools.

Further analysis of political paradigms can likewise account for some of the seemingly contradictory findings of the environmental determinist and rational action schools of voting behavior. This integration requires a brief discussion of the process of paradigm transmittal between generations in a community.

In the scientific community, the dominant scientific paradigm is generally transmitted through formal educational processes, with the paradigms explicitly stated in scientific textbooks. Scientists thus acquire knowledge of the fundamentals of the paradigm at an early stage of their development. The transmittal is conducted implicitly as well as explicitly, and Kuhn points out that "[Scientists can] agree in their identification of a paradigm without agreeing on, or even attempting to produce, a full interpretation or rationalization of it" (p. 44). Thus scientists can identify with and be guided in their activity by a paradigm without complete knowledge of the abstract characteristics and full implications of its content.

This process of transmittal of scientific paradigms bears a remarkable resemblance to the process of "early politicization" described in *The American Voter*, through which the young citizen learns to identify with a political party. One significant difference is that political education has historically been excluded from formal education, and this can perhaps account for the importance of the family in transmitting the paradigm (institutionalized in the political party) to the next generation, as documented in *The American Voter*.

Likewise, the failure of many voters to have explicit views on all political issues and party positions is similar to the behavior of the scientists who accept and identify with the paradigm without complete comprehension of all its ramifications. Within periods of paradigm dominance, one might expect a large proportion of voters (and scientists) to fall into this category. Thus, within the theory of political paradigms, the seemingly nonideological voter is no less rational in his behavior than the scientist.

The theory of political paradigms can account for the identification, by competing behavioral schools of voting behavior, of conscious and subconscious aspects of the voting decision. The existence of the phenomena of party identification and father identification is explained by the fact that the function of paradigm transmittal has been closely tied to the family unit in American society. This can also explain to some extent the predictive ability of socioeconomic class, religion, and place of residence, in the Lazarsfeld studies, since these are family-related characteristics, and the impact of social mobility may have been obscured by the fact that the Lazarsfeld analyses were not based on national samples but on the populations of relatively small and homogeneous subcomponents of the entire political community. The existence of issue-oriented behavior pointed to by the analysts of the rational action school demonstrates that the voting decision reflects more than subconscious, rote loyalty to the party that effected the paradigm shift.

Thus, the theory of political paradigms would hold that both conscious and subconscious elements would be expected to be evident in an individual decision. The cyclical characteristics of ideological attention on the part of the bulk of the community were identified long ago by Edmund Burke: "The bulk of mankind on their part are not excessively curious concerning any [political] theories, whilst they are really happy; and one sure symptom of an ill-conducted state is the propensity of the people to resort to them."[5] Hence, within periods of normal politics one would expect environmental factors to be more important than issue orientations in influencing voting decisions, and the opposite would be true in paradigm-shifting periods.[6]

The role of the parties in institutionalizing paradigms requires further exploration, for American political parties in particular have been noted for their lack of ideological consistency. The theory of political paradigms does not require the ideological consistency of the parties, merely that at certain critical periods of paradigm shifts the parties present the electorate with a choice of ideological paradigms, or concrete puzzle-solutions. Within periods of paradigm dominance, both parties would be expected to exploit the existence of the paradigm. Failure to do so can result in near disaster for a party, as the 1964 election demonstrated. Whether parties have fulfilled the periodic institutionalizations of paradigms required by the theory will be analyzed empirically in a later chapter, although Burnham's description of the unusual ideological conflict and issue-distances accompanying critical elections lends support to the assignment of parties to this role.

5. Edmund Burke, quoted in Boorstin, p. 3, without further citation.
6. While this statement is a logical deduction both from the theory and from impressionistic observations of human behavior (such as Burke's), it cannot be substantiated from survey research works of the kind described in chap. 1, for no survey data exist for any of the elections classified by political analysts as critical. This point will be made explicit in chap. 6.

# 3. A Design for Empirical Analysis
of Political Paradigms

THERE IS no straightforward empirical test for determining the validity of the theory of political paradigms. Kuhn suggested that scientific paradigm shifts could be observed by analyzing contents of references to "basic" works cited most often in the footnotes of scholarly scientific publications and scientific textbooks. The content of the "new" paradigm could then be determined by an analysis of the works cited in the period immediately following the shift.

Unfortunately, a test such as Kuhn proposes is not applicable to political paradigm analysis, as only a very small proportion of the political community publishes its ideological views, and these members can be written off as "small groups of dissenters and alienated intellectuals," as Hofstadter suggests.

A more representative sample of the political community can be obtained by analyzing the American presidential electorate. Lester Milbrath provides twenty-eight citations from social science literature to document the statement that "persons near the center of society are more likely to participate in politics than persons near the periphery."[1] While this obviously contains a bias in considering the electorate as a representative sample of the entire political community, the bias is likely to be toward the "mainstream" of the community and away from the alienated fringes, hence avoiding Hofstadter's criticism.

As noted, empirical analysis of the phenomenon of critical elections has been under way for at least the last two decades. Since critical elections were held to be the exemplary past achievements that consummated the transformation in political paradigms, an empirical analysis of these elections and of their social, economic,

1. *Political Participation* (Chicago: Rand McNally, 1965), pp. 113–14.

and political concomitants can provide a means of examining empirical support for hypotheses derived from the theory of political paradigms. A design for such analyses requires the proposal of empirical techniques to identify critical elections and to identify their social, economic, and political concomitants.

## IDENTIFICATION OF CRITICAL ELECTIONS

Methods for identifying critical elections have generally been of two types: the formation of deductive typologies, based upon a priori selection of the differentiating characteristics of such elections, or the identification of shifts in electoral realignments through inductive analysis of historical voting data.

The first type follows up Key's original suggestion that a satisfactory theory of historical electoral behavior would require the development of a holistic typology of elections, so that one could see clearly the characteristics that differentiate critical elections from the more numerous electoral outcomes that characterize periods of normal conflict. In *The American Voter*, Angus Campbell and his associates contributed to the development of such a typology by defining two additional types of elections: maintaining and deviating. As Figure 1 shows, Gerald M. Pomper later pointed out

Fig. 1.—A classification of presidential elections

|  | | Majority party | |
| --- | --- | --- | --- |
|  |  | Victory | Defeat |
|  | Continuity | "Maintaining" | "Deviating" |
| Electoral cleavage |  |  |  |
|  | Change | "Converting" | "Realigning" (Critical) |

that the Campbell group's trichotomous typology was actually two-dimensional in scope, and he then identified a fourth election type, converting, by filling in the empty cell in their property space.[2] The complete Pomper typology then depends upon two

2. *Elections in America* (New York: Dodd, Mead, 1968), p. 104. For a more detailed discussion of his classification scheme, see Pomper, "Classification of Presidential Elections," *Journal of Politics* 29 (1967): 535–66.

criteria for distinguishing critical elections, the amount of change from the electoral cleavage of the previous election and the outcome of the election for the incumbent party. It does distinguish between converting and realigning (or critical) elections—a distinction that supports the suggestion made earlier that intra-paradigm conflict must be distinguishable from paradigm-shifting conflict—although it does so only on the basis of whether the incumbent party has been returned to the presidency or turned out.

While the Pomper typology of elections appears to fulfill the need for a holistic analysis of electoral alignments as suggested by Key, its primary reliance on subjective definition of the distinguishing characteristics of elections and its assumption of the two-dimensional nature of historical electoral conflict are subject to question. Hugh Douglas Price, in an examination of the methodological problems of arbitrarily selecting criteria for the definition of electoral trends, pointed out that often "In gross outline the trend of historical data is clear. But the inferences to be drawn from it are not so clear and depend substantially upon one's assumptions and criteria."[3] Hence the element of arbitrariness in Pomper's selection of two criteria for differentiating elections may introduce a bias into the typology or, more likely, obscure some additional differentiating characteristics that would be deduced from other potential criteria. The spatial conception of electoral alignments in two dimensions may also be an arbitrary restriction that obscures differentiating phenomena. Recent research by Ronald E. Weber on state party systems indicates that four dimensions of party competition are identifiable at the state level, and this finding certainly casts doubt on the adequacy of a two-dimensional spatial concept of electoral competition at the national level.[4] The Pomper typology must, then, be regarded as a less than definitive method of identifying critical elections.

The second approach to identifying critical realignments of the electorate referred to inductive analysis of historical voting data. This approach was taken by Walter Dean Burnham in his recent monograph, *Critical Elections and the Mainsprings of American*

3. "Micro- and Macro-Politics: Notes on Research Strategy," in *Political Research and Political Theory*, ed. Oliver Garceau (Cambridge: Harvard University Press, 1968), p. 119.
4. "Dimensions of State Party Systems," presented at the 1969 Annual Meeting of the Northeastern Political Science Association, Hartford, Connecticut.

*Politics.* In essence, Burnham forsook the holistic, but subjective, approach to construction of typologies in favor of employing inductive statistical techniques to identify "cutting points" of transition from one system of electoral politics to another. He argued that attention should be focused on any rapid and compressed realignment of the electorate, and criticized distinctions between converting and critical realignments as "superfluous typologies" which serve to "make analysis perhaps more complex than is necessary."

Burnham applied two types of statistical tests to the historical Democratic percentage of the two-party vote. The first, the Ezekiel-Fox discontinuity test, is a variant of linear regression analysis.[5] Burnham took sequences of ten presidential elections at a time. The elections were identified in the regression analysis by dummy variables, the first five elections having a value of zero, the rest a value of one. The regression was then performed on the Democratic percentage of the vote. In this analysis, the first five elections are considered one period and the second five another. Ezekiel and Fox then argue that "A significant net regression coefficient implies a significant change in the relationship from one period to the other" (p. 344). Burnham applied this procedure to all possible sets of ten contiguous elections and identified four periods of critical realignment (pp. 13–18).

The second test employed by Burnham was a simple student's *t* difference of means test. Again considering sequences of ten elections, Burnham argued that a statistically significant difference of means between the two five-election subgroups indicated a significant change in the alignment of the electorate. The results of this analysis tended to confirm the findings of the discontinuity tests, and the same four critical periods were identified (p. 16).

While Burnham's techniques are inviting because they lack subjectivity, they are not without undesirable characteristics. The analysis requires the existence of ten contiguous elections in which the popular vote was taken. Using Burnham's convention of identifying midpoint years of these sequences as the cutting points, this means that the earliest period that can be tested has as a midpoint 1846, and the latest, 1950. In addition, Burnham's focus on periods, rather than specific elections, somewhat obscures the

5. Mordecai Ezekiel and Karl A. Fox, *Methods of Correlation and Regression Analysis*, 3d ed. (New York: Wiley, 1959), pp. 343–44.

precise identification of a single election as critical. While earlier research by Duncan MacRae and James A. Meldrun pointed to the existence of critical periods preceding critical elections,[6] thus lending some support to Burnham's period analysis approach, both Key's original theory and the theory of political paradigms require that one election be identified at which the paradigm shift is effected. Thus Burnham's approach is not directly applicable to a test of political paradigms. And, finally, in forsaking the holistic approach, Burnham leaves unanswered the question of precisely what electoral characteristics distinguish paradigm-shifting elections from normal politics.

Thus neither of the methods previously used to identify critical elections appears definitive enough to employ in a test of the theory of political paradigms. A new method will be proposed which incorporates desirable elements of both the holistic and inductive approaches, while minimizing the effect of their undesirable characteristics.

### INDUCTIVE DEFINITION OF ELECTION TYPES

The method chosen to identify critical elections involves the use of multivariate techniques of statistical analysis to develop an inductive typology of presidential elections. These techniques will allow the use of a relatively large number of differentiating characteristics, and will permit an $n$-dimensional spatial conception of the construct of electoral alignment. In addition, the inductive nature of these techniques lessens reliance on subjective choice of distinguishing criteria. The specific multivariate techniques to be employed are those of alpha factor analysis to estimate differentiating dimensions of elections, and hierarchical cluster analysis to group the elections into natural clusters or types based upon the differentiating dimensions identified. The typology developed in this manner will therefore share the holistic quality of the Pomper typology and the inductive objectivity of the Burnham analyses.

Alpha factor analysis, described in detail in Appendix 1, was developed to generalize from a nonrandom sample of variables that measure aspects of a phenomenological construct to the uni-

6. "Critical Elections in Illinois: 1888–1958," *American Political Science Review* 54 (1960): 669–83.

verse of content of that construct, based upon the information contained in a population of cases. In this analysis the required population of cases is defined as all presidential elections within the period of the modern party system, i.e., since 1860.[7] (The decision to eliminate earlier elections was based partly upon the design's need for concomitant social, economic, and political data, practically none of which is available for the period prior to 1860.) The nonrandom sample of variables includes twenty-seven measures of the distribution of the electorate; these will be identified in chapter 4. And the phenomenological construct to be generalized to is the dimensionality of electoral alignment. The alpha factors extracted from the twenty-seven variables in this analysis are then presented as the "best" available approximations of the "true" differentiating dimensions of electoral alignment (see Appendix 1).

The identification of differentiating dimensions of electoral alignment is only the first step in the construction of the inductive typology of elections. The second step consists of the actual formation of the election groups or types based upon an analysis of the factor scores of the individual elections on each of the differentiating elections identified.[8]

The technique employed in the development of election types is hierarchical cluster analysis. This technique, based on an algorithm proposed by Joe H. Ward, Jr.,[9] initially considers each

7. Research supporting the dating of the modern party system from ca. 1860 to the present can be found in such sources as Richard P. McCormick, "Political Development and the Second Party System," and Walter Dean Burnham, "Party Systems and the Political Process," both in *The American Party Systems,* eds. William N. Chambers and Walter Dean Burnham (New York: Oxford University Press, 1967).

8. The alpha factor analysis conducted here utilized the computer program described in Norman H. Nie, Dale H. Bent, and C. Hadlai Hull, *SPSS: Statistical Package for the Social Sciences* (New York: McGraw-Hill, 1970). Unfortunately, the SPSS factor analysis program permits the computation of factor scores only from factor matrices rotated to simple structure. In order to generate factor scores for each election from the alpha factors, an original computer program was written in MATLAN, employing the procedure specified by M. S. Bartlett for estimation of factor scores. See Donald F. Morrison, *Multivariate Statistical Methods* (New York: McGraw-Hill, 1967), p. 293.

9. "Hierarchical Grouping to Optimize an Objective Function," *American Statistical Association Journal* 58 (1963): 236–44. The computer program used to employ Ward's algorithm was written by Phillip Bell and Stephen Gladin, graduate students in the Departments of Industrial and Systems Engineering, and Geography, respectively, at the University of Florida.

election as a separate group. Then, in a stepwise fashion, elections are grouped on the basis of their factor scores until all elections are placed in a single group. The grouping criterion employed is to join those elections, or groups of elections, whose union will result in the smallest increase in within-group heterogeneity (variance). The groups thus formed at each step will be the most homogeneous groupings possible. The groups formed at each step of the process are defined by the algorithm, and a decision must be made as to the number of groups to be employed in the typology. The criterion for selecting the number of groups to be employed in this study was the widely used procedure suggested by Ward, i.e., to select the smallest number of groups formed just prior to a sharp loss in within-group homogeneity (a sharp increase in within-group variance). The rationale behind this criterion is that the drop in homogeneity indicates a "natural" cutoff point in terms of selecting the number of groups to be included in a typology as it indicates that a greater than normal loss of group individuality would occur by breaking off an additional group.

The application of the alpha factor analysis and hierarchical clustering techniques to historical election data provides an inductive methodology for development of a holistic typology of elections. This is the first stage of the proposed empirical analysis of the theory of political paradigms.

## SOCIETAL CONCOMITANTS OF ELECTION TYPES

Examination of empirical support for hypotheses derived from the theory of political paradigms requires the identification of social, economic, and political concomitants of the election types. The method selected for identifying such phenomena is a stepwise multiple discriminant analysis of election types, based not upon the factor scores from which they were originally grouped, but rather upon fifty-four measures of societal change (discussed in chapter 5).

Discriminant function analysis is a statistical technique originally developed to classify an individual with known characteristics into one of several groups, the characteristics of whose members are also known. The technique is actually a variant of Hotelling's $T^2$ multivariate difference of means test, and was adapted by R. A.

Fisher as a classificatory measure.[10] Later, the technique was further adapted to a stepwise computational format in order that the characteristics that discriminated the groups could be determined in their relative order of importance. Several criteria for entering variables into the stepwise function have been developed, and the one employed here is to enter the variable which, when partialed on previously entered variables, if any, has the highest multiple correlation with the groups.[11] Selection of this criterion controls for the effect of intercolinearity among the original fifty-four variables included in the analysis.

As noted, the original characteristics on which the electoral types were formed are not included in the discriminant analysis. The groupings of elections are independent of any consideration of the variables in the factor analysis. The discriminant analysis based on the fifty-four measures of societal change will then identify which societal change variables best discriminate the election types, which leads to an interpretation of the specific phenomena concomitant to electoral outcomes.

Two forms of interpretation are involved. The first is an interpretation of the discriminant function coefficients of the variables that distinguish the types. This enables an interpretation of what social trends are associated with election types. The second interpretation involves the computation of scores for the individual elections in order to determine the relationships of the election types to the discriminating phenomenon.

This application will complete the empirical analyses of the distribution of the electorate in presidential elections, and of social, economic, and political phenomena that are concomitant to types of electoral distributions.

## HYPOTHESES ON POLITICAL PARADIGMS

This research design for the empirical analysis of political paradigms will conclude with the statement of five hypotheses derived from the discussion in chapter 2; if supported by the empirical

10. For a discussion of this adaptation see Morrison, pp. 130–32.
11. The multiple discriminant program employed was "BMDO7M: Stepwise Discriminant Analysis," in W. J. Dixon, ed., *BMD: Biomedical Computer Programs* (Berkeley: University of California Press, 1967). A description of other criteria available for entering variables into the discriminant function is included in that reference.

analyses discussed in this chapter, these would lend support to the validity of the theory of political paradigms:

Hypothesis 1: Paradigm-shifting elections and normal party competition elections should be typologically distinct in the configurations of their electorate.

Hypothesis 2: Paradigm-shifting elections should coincide with some societal crisis which inspires the attentiveness of the electorate.

Hypothesis 3: The victorious party in paradigm-shifting elections should have proposed a new paradigm, ideologically opposed to the previous one.

Hypothesis 4: Periods following paradigm shifts should be marked by a return to normal party competition.

Hypothesis 5: Periods prior to paradigm shifts should show some distortion of normal party competition as the electorate becomes aware of anomalies to which the dominant paradigm cannot respond.

# 4. An Inductive Typology of Elections

THE METHODS described in chapter 3 will now be used to construct an inductive typology of presidential elections for the period 1860–1968. As noted, Pomper had two differentiating characteristics in his typology, the amount of change in partisan support from the previous election and the outcome of the election for the incumbent party. Burnham's inductive analysis used only the Democratic percentage of the vote. In this analysis, twenty-seven differentiating characteristics of elections, shown in Table 1, will be applied, and the reasons for their inclusion will be discussed.

Both Pomper and Burnham agreed that change in party support is an important differentiating characteristic of elections, but there are two ways of measuring such change. Burnham compared levels of support for a party. Pomper measured the change from the previous election in the amount of support received by the party. The distinction is between levels of support or change in levels of support. Both types of measurements are included in this analysis.

The first four variables measure the percentage of support and the percentage change in support for the two major parties, winning and losing. The measurement of support for winning and losing parties, rather than for Republican and Democratic, was used because, consistent with Pomper's approach, the phenomenon under investigation is electoral realignment from a period of party dominance, regardless of which party happens to be dominant at that moment. Hence, a realigning election would be marked by a sharp increase in vote for the winner and a similar decline for the loser. If the variables instead measured Republican and Democratic percentages of the vote, realignments would be broken down into Republican and Democratic realignments, and that is not the purpose of the analysis.

27

TABLE 1.—DIFFERENTIATING CHARACTERISTICS OF ELECTIONS

1. Per cent of vote for winning party
2. Change in per cent of vote for winning party[a]
3. Per cent of vote for runner-up party
4. Change in per cent of vote for runner-up party
5. Per cent of vote for all third parties
6. Change in per cent of vote for all third parties
7. Number of parties receiving at least 1 per cent of vote
8. Change in number of parties receiving at least 1 per cent of vote
9. National margin of victory
10. Incumbent party turnover or re-election
11. Number of immediately preceding elections won by winning party
12. Number of immediately following elections won by winning party
13. Number of preceding 5 elections won by winning party
14. Number of following 5 elections won by winning party
15. Per cent change in aggregate turnout
16. Per cent of states carried by winning party
17. Change in per cent of states carried by winning party
18. Per cent of states switching party allegiance
19. State voting shift distribution: mean
20. State voting shift distribution: standard deviation
21. State voting shift distribution: skewness
22. State margin of victory distribution: mean
23. State margin of victory distribution: standard deviation
24. State margin of victory distribution: skewness
25. Per cent of electoral college vote for winning party
26. Per cent of electoral college vote for runner-up party
27. Per cent of electoral college vote for all third parties

SOURCES: for elections in the period 1860–1960, Svend Petersen, *A Statistical History of the American Presidential Elections* (New York: Ungar, 1963); for the elections of 1964 and 1968, Richard C. Scammon, comp., *America Votes 8* (Washington: Governmental Affairs Institute, 1968).

a. All "change" variables measure shifts from the immediately preceding election.

The fifth and sixth variables measure the level of support and change in level of support for all third parties. These variables are intended to operationalize support for elements espousing issues that are outside the framework of the issues encompassed by the two major parties. Whether this support was aggregated in a single third party or dispersed among several parties is made clear by variables 7 and 8, which measure the number of parties that received at least 1 per cent of the vote and the change in the number of such parties.

The ninth variable measures the closeness of the competition at the national level, which relates to Pomper's notion of change in electoral cleavage, and the tenth measures whether or not the incumbent party was turned out, the other criterion used by Pomper.[1] Variables 11–14 go beyond the previous election in measuring the history of success of the winning party: variables 11 and 13 measure the number of immediately preceding elections carried by the current winner and the number of the preceding 5 elections it won; variables 12 and 14 measure similar phenomena for succeeding elections.[2]

Variable 15 measures the percentage change in aggregate turnout from the preceding election, a phenomenon that Burnham subjected to secondary analysis in support of the results generated by his examination of the Democratic percentage of the vote.[3]

These first fifteen variables all provide measures of the behavior of the electorate at the aggregate or national level. Several analysts have considered the role of individual states in effecting realignments, since presidents are not elected by aggregate distribution of the popular vote, but rather by their victories in sufficiently populous states to win them a majority in the electoral college.[4] A comprehensive typology of elections should include some data on voting patterns at the state level, and variables 16–24 measure changes in these patterns.

Variable 16, an obvious choice, measures the percentage of states carried by the winner; variable 17 measures the change in this

1. The tenth variable is a "dummy" variable which is coded as 1 if the election involved a turnover of party and 0 if the incumbent party was returned to office.

2. Obviously no data were available for the 1968 election on variable 12 since there are no data on following elections, and likewise no data were available for the elections of 1952, 1956, 1960, 1964, and 1968 on variable 14 which required the existence of five following elections. In the conduct of the factor analysis, these cases were identified as missing data, and were not included in the computation of correlation coefficients between variables 12 and 14 and the other variables. Data for these elections were included in the computation of all other correlation coefficients, however. For the precise manner in which missing data are handled in the SPSS factor analysis program, see Nie, Bent, and Hull, p. 236, "Option 2." Examination of factor scores of these elections indicates that while some distortion is evident as the result of the missing data, the distortion is not great enough to bias the placement of these elections into the types formed by the hierarchical cluster analysis.

3. *Critical Elections*, pp. 18–21.

4. For the importance of historical voting patterns in analyzing electoral alignments, see Key and Munger, "Social Determinism and Electoral Decision." The importance of sectional deviation from national trends in definition of realignments is given by Charles Sellers in "The Equilibrium Cycle in Two Party Politics," *Public Opinion Quarterly* 29 (1965): 16–38.

percentage from the previous election. Variable 18 measures the percentage of states that switched allegiance (hence their electoral vote) from one party to another.

Variables 19–21 are attempts to measure in individual states the deviance from the mean or average state shift in the vote for the winner in each election. For each election, there is a distribution of elements measuring voting shifts by state to or away from the winning party. Variable 19 presents the mean of the distribution, or the average per cent shift in state vote. Deviation from this average shift by individual states is measured by variable 20, the standard deviation of the distribution. A large standard deviation would indicate that change in support for the winning party varied greatly among the individual states. Variable 21 measures the degree to which the deviation was skewed in a positive or negative direction away from the mean.

Variables 22–24 measure similar characteristics of distributions of the margin of victory (or defeat) of the nationally victorious party in each state. Variable 22 presents the mean state margin of victory (defeat), variable 23 measures the standard deviation of the states about the mean, and variable 24 measures skewness about the mean.

The last three variables measure the electoral vote for winning, runner-up, and all third parties. The electoral vote provides a method of weighting a party's ability to carry individual states by the population of those states. As such, it integrates the measures of aggregate and state distributions of the vote. Since a party's ability to remain in power rests on its ability to carry states large enough to garner a majority of the electoral college vote, a typology of elections should include measures of the party's success at doing so.

These 27 variables include more detailed observations of the differentiating phenomena incorporated in the Burnham and Pomper methods and observations of additional phenomena relevant to the differentiation of electoral alignments. Measures of these variables for the elections from 1860 to 1968 were then subjected to an alpha factor analysis as described in chapter 3.

As Table 2 indicates, 6 alpha factors were extracted from the 27 variables and these 6 factors contained more than 76 per cent of the total variance. The selection of the number of factors to be extracted was made by application of the three criteria recommended for alpha factor analysis applications by R. J. Rummel,[5] shown in Figure 2.

The three criteria suggested by Rummel are the eigenvalue-one, discontinuity, and scree tests. As Figure 2 indicates, the eigenvalue-one cutoff occurs at eight factors, indicating that the number of factors to be extracted lies in this general area. However, a discontinuity in the slope of the curve occurs in going from the sixth to the seventh factor, while the slope is relatively constant from the seventh factor on. This indicates that, according to the discontinuity criterion, only six factors should be extracted. The scree test, which derives its name from the geological distinction of a mountain range from its scree—the debris that has eroded from the range and lies at its base—holds that after a certain point the curve plotted in Figure 2 will assume a constant slope that will become asymptotic to the x-axis. This line appears to begin immediately following the discontinuity observed between factors 6 and 7, thus also suggesting that six factors are to be extracted. Since these six factors cumulatively account for a rather large proportion of the total variance, almost 77 per cent, and since inclusion of factors 7 and 8 would increase the amount of variance included only by 5 and 4 per cent, respectively, the six-factor cut-off point suggested by the discontinuity and scree test was adopted.

Another method of assessing confidence in the factors extracted is to examine the amount of variance of each individual variable that is accounted for in the six factors. The percentage of variance accounted for in each variable is given in the column headed "Communalities" at the far right of Table 2. Examination of the communalities shows that most of the variables have a substantial proportion of their variance included in the six factors. Only variable 15, the percentage change in aggregate turnout, goes virtually unexplained. One possible reason is that sharp shifts in turnout may be generally accounted for by unique characteristics of individual elections, such as the weather or the personal charisma of the candidates; hence, variance in turnout would be associated with unique variance not included in the alpha factors, which describe only common or shared variance. The relatively large number of high communality values tends to lend additional support to the selection of six factors.

5. *Applied Factor Analysis* (Evanston: Northwestern University Press, 1970), pp. 354–67.

TABLE 2.—ALPHA FACTOR LOADINGS

| | Normal competition | Realignment: multiparty | Realignment: two-party | Deviating | Maintaining | Consensus of states | Communalities |
|---|---|---|---|---|---|---|---|
| 1. Per cent of vote—winner | −.65 | −.56 | .29 | −.20 | −.19 | −.05 | .90 |
| 2. Change in per cent of vote—winner | −.62 | .29 | .51 | .22 | .09 | −.08 | .79 |
| 3. Per cent of vote—runner-up | .48 | −.51 | .42 | .38 | .39 | .05 | .96 |
| 4. Change in per cent of vote—runner-up | .06 | −.24 | −.32 | .21 | −.02 | −.06 | .21 |
| 5. Per cent of vote—all third parties | .07 | .72 | −.51 | −.12 | −.17 | .03 | .83 |
| 6. Change in per cent of vote—all third parties | .21 | .40 | −.22 | −.40 | −.20 | .41 | .62 |
| 7. Number of parties with at least 1 per cent of vote | .28 | .42 | −.23 | .02 | −.34 | −.16 | .45 |
| 8. Change in number of parties | .37 | .35 | .04 | −.26 | −.06 | .37 | .46 |
| 9. National margin of victory | −.77 | −.02 | −.11 | −.43 | −.45 | −.05 | .99 |
| 10. Turnover (+) or re-election (−) | .04 | .69 | .26 | .37 | −.24 | .17 | .77 |
| 11. Number preceding elections won | .26 | −.42 | −.08 | −.26 | .13 | .03 | .33 |
| 12. Number following elections won | −.30 | .30 | −.01 | .04 | .27 | −.02 | .26 |
| 13. Number elections won—preceding 20 years | .28 | −.29 | .17 | −.33 | −.06 | −.03 | .31 |
| 14. Number elections won—following 20 years | −.05 | .13 | −.01 | −.02 | .46 | .04 | .23 |
| 15. Per cent change in aggregate turnout | −.01 | −.01 | .08 | .07 | −.14 | −.01 | .03 |
| 16. Per cent of states carried by winner | −.85 | −.25 | −.13 | −.19 | −.01 | .23 | .88 |
| 17. Change in per cent of states carried by winner | −.51 | .04 | −.07 | −.12 | .01 | −.17 | .31 |
| 18. Per cent of states switching parties | −.01 | .22 | .30 | −.01 | −.11 | .17 | .19 |
| 19. State voting shift distribution—mean | −.68 | .33 | .47 | .31 | −.04 | −.09 | .89 |
| 20. State voting shift distribution—standard deviation | −.01 | .31 | .19 | −.19 | .25 | −.18 | .26 |
| 21. State voting shift distribution—skewness | −.35 | .16 | −.39 | .40 | .04 | −.13 | .48 |
| 22. State margin of victory distribution—mean | −.70 | −.29 | −.14 | −.01 | −.18 | .38 | .77 |
| 23. State margin of victory distribution—standard deviation | −.08 | .20 | −.16 | −.15 | −.13 | −.28 | .19 |

TABLE 2—*Continued*

| | | | | | | | |
|---|---|---|---|---|---|---|---|
| 24. State margin of victory distribution—skewness | .01 | .06 | −.28 | .30 | .07 | .31 | .27 |
| 25. Per cent of electoral vote—winner | −.89 | −.25 | −.17 | −.20 | .08 | .22 | .97 |
| 26. Per cent of electoral vote—runner-up | .86 | .05 | .19 | .28 | −.17 | −.23 | .94 |
| 27. Per cent of electoral vote—all third parties | .15 | .54 | −.03 | −.16 | .21 | .01 | .38 |
| Alpha coefficient of generalizability | .67 | .63 | .50 | .48 | .46 | .34 | |
| Behavior domain validity coefficient | .82 | .79 | .71 | .69 | .68 | .58 | |
| Associated per cent of common variance | 22.7 | 20.4 | 15.5 | 14.8 | 14.5 | 12.0 | 100.0 |
| Associated per cent of total variance | 17.5 | 15.7 | 11.9 | 11.4 | 11.2 | 9.2 | 76.9 |

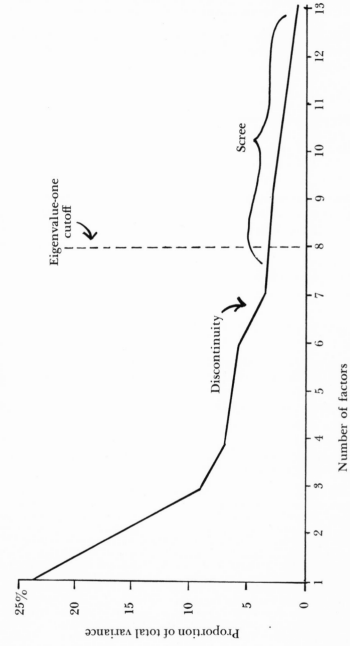

Fig. 2.—Selection of the number of factors

Finally, one may judge the validity of the alpha factors as true measures of phenomena common to the universe of the construct of electoral alignment by examination of the alpha and behavior domain validity coefficients of the individual factors, provided at the bottom of Table 2. The relatively large behavior domain validity coefficients indicate that the factors are close to "a perfect criterion measure of the property X, as operationally defined,"[6] although the .58 coefficient of the sixth factor does indicate that the measurement of the phenomena associated with that factor could be somewhat improved.

Having assessed the validity of the alpha factors extracted, and found them satisfactory in terms of the several criteria discussed, there remains only to define "the property X" which each of the factors is attempting to describe. This is done by an examination of the factor loadings and then by "naming" the factors in terms of the property which they are thought to define. (The factor names appear at the head of each column of the factor loading matrix in Table 2.)

The first factor has been named normal competition after an examination of its variable loadings. The phenomena described by this factor closely approximate the conditions postulated by Anthony Downs as occurring during normal periods of ideological stability.[7] The factor loadings indicate a split of the vote between the two major parties, with a slight margin of victory. Competition in the individual states was also close and historical state party allegiances remained stable. Third party activity was not evident to any measurable degree. Hence, the factor with the greatest gen-

---

6. Robert C. Tryon, "Reliability and Behavior Domain Validity: Reformulation and Historical Critique," *Psychological Bulletin* 54 (1957): 229–49.

7. *An Economic Theory of Democracy* (New York: Harper, 1957). Downs' conception of normality has been criticized as "simplistic" due to its unidimensional representation of ideological conflict; see Donald E. Stokes, "Spatial Models of Party Competition, in *Elections and the Political Order*, eds. Angus Campbell, Phillip E. Converse, Warren E. Miller, and Donald E. Stokes (New York: Wiley, 1966), pp. 161–79. But his line of reasoning has been extended into n–dimensional frames of reference; see Otto A. Davis, Melvin J. Hinich, and Peter C. Ordeshook, "An Expository Development of a Mathematical Model of the Electoral Process," *American Political Science Review* 64 (1970): 426–48. As economists have long employed two-dimensional summary representations of multidimensional phenomena as teaching devices, the heuristic value of the Downsian conception of normality is held to be only marginally diminished by its unidimensional base.

eralizability tends to describe conditions that have been associated with periods of normal politics.

The second factor, labeled realignment: multiparty, incorporates elements of critical realignment with elements of third party activity. A shift of votes from the second major party to the winning party and to third parties occurs, perhaps indicating the failure of the second major party to disassociate itself from a rejected paradigm. State historical voting patterns are shown to be in turmoil on this dimension, and a turnover of party is highly likely. In addition, the winning party had not been generally successful in the period preceding the election, but was somewhat more likely to enjoy success in the years following, particularly in the next election. Third party activity was likely to be successful in capturing electoral college votes.

The third factor also contains elements of realignment, but differs from the second primarily in the absence of third party activity. Like the second factor, historical state voting patterns are upset, with the shifts larger in magnitude and with less deviation of the individual states from the average substantial shift. At the national level, votes are redistributed, away from second and third parties to the winning party. Evidence of shifts in state party allegiance is also indicated. This factor has also been designated as describing realignment, but is distinguished from the second factor by limiting the electoral conflict to the two major parties, with the winning party clearly emerging dominant.

The fourth and fifth factors appear to identify patterns of electoral conflict similar to those defined by Campbell and associates. The fourth factor, termed deviating, is characterized by stable state party allegiance, a close national margin of victory, a lack of dominance by the winning party in periods preceding or following the election, and a likely turnover of parties. This seems to fit closely the conception of a deviating election in which the dominant party is upset by the second major party but recovers soon thereafter. The fifth factor is likewise characterized by a stable electoral cleavage and a close margin of victory, while the result is more likely to be a victory for the incumbent party, hence the designation, maintaining. These two factors may identify divergent patterns of conflict in otherwise normal elections.

The sixth and final factor is more difficult to interpret due to its generally low factor loadings, as indicated by its lower behavior domain validity coefficient compared to the other factors. Some recognizable features are an increase in the number of third parties, a large average state margin of victory for the winner, with only slight deviation of individual states from the average margin, and concomitant increases in the percentage of states carried by the winner and the percentage of states switching party allegiances. This appears to describe the detraction of support from the second major parties to third parties in a period of normal conflict. The net result of these phenomena would appear as the winning party achieving a consensus of the individual states, hence the term consensus of states for this factor.

These six factors then have been inductively developed from the 27 original measures of electoral distribution cited in Table 1. The employment of Cronbach's alpha coefficient of generalizability as a criterion for selection of the factor loading matrix assures that these factors come as close as possible to measuring the differentiating dimensions of the theoretical construct of electoral alignment. Factor scores for each election on each of these factors would then seem to be the most appropriate measures upon which to base a holistic typology of presidential elections.

These scores were calculated, and were used to develop a typology of elections by application of a hierarchical cluster analysis. The factor scores and the groups of elections developed are shown in Table 3.[8] Seven groups or types of elections were formed. The criterion used to determine the number of groups to be included in the typology was the one suggested by Ward (pp. 236–44), to select the smallest number of groups formed just prior to a sharp loss in within-group homogeneity, or an increase in within-group variance. Figure 3 charts the changes in between-group variance at stages of groupings from two groups to thirteen groups. A sharp decline in the slope of this line would then indicate a concurrent increase in within-group variance; hence the criterion as stated in the chart is to select the smallest number of groups just prior to a sharp loss in between-group variance.

As indicated in Figure 2, one possible choice was to include just two groups in the typology, as a sharp decline in between-group variance occurred in going from two to three groups. Such a de-

8. The computation of factor scores was conducted by an original computer program, written in MATLAN, which employed Bartlett's formula for factor score estimation (see Morrison, p. 293).

TABLE 3.—FACTOR SCORES BY ELECTION GROUP

| Election Groups | Factors | | | | | |
|---|---|---|---|---|---|---|
| | Normal competition | Realignment: multiparty | Realignment: two-party | Deviating | Maintaining | Consensus of states |
| 1. Realigning elections | | | | | | |
| Type A: two-party realignments | | | | | | |
| 1896 | .53 | .60 | 1.53 | -.15 | .49 | -.84 |
| 1920 | -1.14 | .53 | 1.42 | -.05 | -2.72 | -.33 |
| 1932 | -1.68 | .93 | 1.66 | .45 | -.29 | 1.78 |
| Type A group mean | -.76 | .69 | 1.54 | .08 | -.84 | .20 |
| Type B: multiparty realignments | | | | | | |
| 1860 | -.23 | 3.81 | -.69 | -.99 | 1.62 | -2.14 |
| 1912 | -.44 | 1.83 | -3.28 | 1.19 | -1.15 | 2.33 |
| Type B group mean | -.33 | 2.82 | -1.98 | .10 | .24 | .09 |
| 2. Maintaining elections | | | | | | |
| Type C: reconstituting elections | | | | | | |
| 1868 | .42 | -.92 | -.13 | -.35 | .88 | .56 |
| 1872 | -.51 | -.45 | .22 | -.75 | 1.04 | .67 |
| 1936 | -1.49 | -.95 | -.74 | -.56 | .64 | 1.14 |
| 1940 | -.20 | -1.50 | -1.47 | .41 | .37 | .99 |
| 1944 | .01 | -1.08 | -.73 | .06 | .74 | 1.16 |
| 1956 | -.52 | -.79 | .18 | -1.00 | .30 | .69 |
| 1964 | -1.27 | -1.51 | 1.57 | -2.02 | .23 | .01 |
| Type C group mean | -.51 | -1.03 | -.16 | -.60 | .42 | .74 |

## TABLE 3—Continued

| | | | | | |
|---|---|---|---|---|---|
| **Type D: restabilizing elections** | | | | | |
| 1864 | -1.84 | -.39 | -.62 | 1.28 | 2.52 | -2.06 |
| 1916 | .22 | -.55 | -.78 | 3.29 | -1.18 | -1.99 |
| Type D group mean | -.86 | -.47 | -.70 | 2.28 | .67 | -2.02 |
| **Type E: converting elections** | | | | | |
| 1900 | .23 | -.36 | -.27 | .31 | .67 | -1.77 |
| 1904 | -.22 | -.16 | .13 | -.91 | -.99 | -1.57 |
| 1908 | .69 | -.72 | -.87 | -.38 | -.07 | -.95 |
| 1924 | .11 | -.08 | -1.60 | -1.83 | -1.98 | -1.36 |
| 1928 | -1.05 | -.85 | -.09 | .03 | -.07 | -1.34 |
| Type E group mean | -.05 | -.43 | -.54 | -.55 | -.49 | -1.40 |
| **3. Deviating elections** | | | | | |
| **Type F: deviating elections** | | | | | |
| 1880 | 1.24 | -.40 | .19 | -.08 | .60 | -.24 |
| 1884 | 1.05 | -.12 | .08 | 1.97 | -1.10 | .82 |
| 1888 | 1.12 | -.10 | .31 | .67 | -.12 | .33 |
| 1892 | .91 | .64 | -.48 | .22 | .14 | .66 |
| 1952 | -1.34 | .06 | .46 | 1.77 | .29 | .22 |
| 1960 | .84 | .41 | 1.62 | .84 | .17 | .66 |
| Type F group mean | .64 | .08 | .36 | .90 | .01 | .41 |
| **Type G: disintegrative elections** | | | | | |
| 1876 | 1.98 | -1.17 | .35 | -.50 | -.84 | .25 |
| 1948 | 1.69 | -.10 | .52 | -2.14 | .47 | .63 |
| 1968 | 1.04 | 2.00 | 1.44 | -.94 | .94 | 1.60 |
| Type G group mean | 1.57 | .25 | .77 | -1.19 | .19 | .82 |

Fig. 3.—Selection of the number of groups

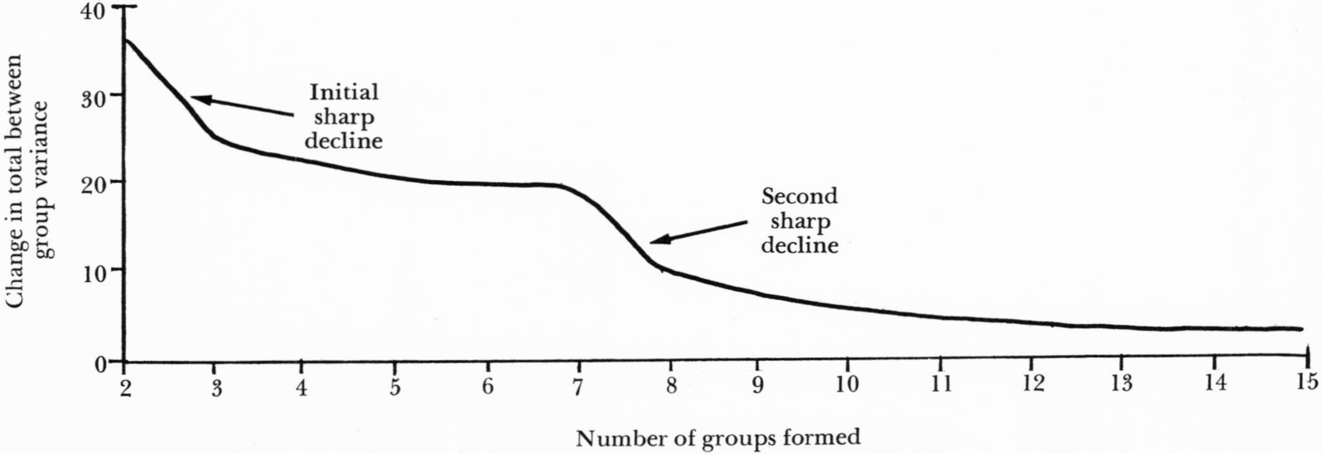

cision, however, would have resulted in a typology consisting of one group of nine elections and another group of nineteen, for which no theoretical basis for division was immediately evident. After deciding that two groups would not provide a theoretically interpretable typology, the next sharp decline occurred in going from the seventh to the eighth group. The decline in between-group variance in going from three groups to seven followed a relatively constant slope, as shown in Figure 2. However, a relatively sharp decline occurred in going from seven to eight groups, after which the curve again assumed a relatively constant slope. After examination of the electoral typology formed by the seven groups, it was selected as being in accord with both Ward's empirical criterion and the criterion of theoretical interpretability. An additional indication of the "tightness" of the groups is that only 36.7 per cent of the total variance in the electoral groups is within-group variance.

In the same manner as interpreting the alpha factors, names were applied to each of the election groups by examining the patterns evident in the factor scores from which the groups were derived. In Table 3, the seven groups were divided into three broader generic categories, realigning, maintaining, and deviating, in a manner that will be explained.

Two types of elections were distinguished in the category headed realigning elections. The first, labeled Type A: two-party realignments, contains three elections with fairly high scores on factor 2 and even higher scores on factor 3. The combination of these high scores and the low scores on the normal competition factor clearly classifies these elections as critical as defined in chapter 2 by Key and Burnham. The second, Type B: multi-party realignments, also had extremely high scores on factor 2 and also scored negatively on normal competition, but, unlike Type A, had negative scores on the third factor. This group of elections thus appears dominated by the elements that composed the second factor, "realignment: multiparty," hence the designation of these elections as multiparty realignments.

The next three types of elections have been generically classified as maintaining. Type C: reconstituting had negative scores on the normal competition and realignment factors, but positive on the maintaining and consensus of states factors. This pattern seems to be one in which the incumbent party is returned to office with an even greater consensus of states than in its previous victory, hence the term reconstituting. Type D: restabilizing elections is composed of only the two elections that immediately followed type B: multiparty realignments. These elections, while themselves having negative scores on realignment dimensions, had positive scores on the deviating dimension even though no turnover of party was involved. The unique nature of these elections seems to have been the ability to "restabilize" the electorate into stable two-party competition, after a strong third party challenge in the previous election. The decline of third party vote would account for the positive deviating scores, although the maintenance of the previously victorious party in office justifies categorizing these elections as maintaining. The existence of this type of election may reflect the ability of the major parties to respond quickly to issues capable of generating strong third party support. Type E: converting elections also has negative scores on the realignment dimensions, but is generally negative on the deviating, maintaining, and normal competition factors as well. These elections might be described as "anti-alignments," for while they generally returned the incumbent party to office, they neither increased or decreased net support for the party. These elections are believed to be associated with alignments which are generally unstable but are maintained by shifting appeal to divergent groups of voters, hence maintaining a minimal winning coalition. They have been termed converting after the ability to convert a previously victorious coalition, without the continuity of electoral cleavage generally associated with lasting alignments.

The last two electoral types have been classified as deviating. Type F: deviating elections has positive scores on the normal competition and deviating dimensions. Some realignment is evident, as would be required to effect the turnover of parties, and the shifts in support of states are evident in the positive scores on the consensus of states dimension. These elections then fit the definition of deviating elections described by Pomper, i.e., a turnover of party in a period of normal competition. The final group, type G: disintegrative elections, follows the same general pattern as deviating elections, but is distinguished from type F by negative scores on the deviating factor. These scores no doubt result from the greater than usual shifts in historical state voting patterns evidenced in these elections. The three elections in this group were all marked by the introduction of third party movements: the Greenbacks in 1876, the Dixiecrats in 1948, and the American Independents in 1968. Each of these movements had regional bases of power, the Greenbacks in the Midwest and the others in the South. The shifts in the historical voting patterns of the states supporting these movements were sufficient to distinguish these elections from normal deviating elections, and actually only the 1968 election effected a change in party control of the presidency. The term disintegrative has been applied to these elections to suggest the breakdown of the previous electoral cleavage without the concurrent production of a stable replacement. Both the 1876 and 1948 elections were followed by normal deviating elections as electoral cleavages were somewhat restabilized. What will follow the 1968 disintegration of the previous electoral coalition is, of course, unknown.[9]

There are reasons for the generic classifications of the seven election types as realigning, maintaining, or deviating. While it is, of course, impossible to represent a six-dimensional typology of elections in two-dimensional space (as the Pomper typology shown in Figure 1), Figure 4 shows the relative position of the electoral groupings on two of the more important phenomena identified, realignment and normal competition. For our purposes here, the figures plotted on the y-axis represent a realignment index compiled by computing the mean scores of all elections in a group on factors two and three, which were said to jointly describe the phenomenon of realignment. The x-axis merely describes the group mean scores on the normal competition factor. Hence, Figure 4 contains a summary of information from the three dimensions that were found to have the greatest generalizability. Division of Figure 4 into quadrants by the dotted lines perpendicular to the zero points of both scales displays the relationships upon which the categorizations of the groups are based. Groups A and B fall into the upper left, or realignment, quadrant. This indicates positive mean scores on the realignment index and negative mean scores on the normal competition index or the general conditions of realignment discussed. Groups C, D, and E all fall into the lower

9. As this work was already in the process of publication, data for the 1972 election was not included in the analysis. While any classification of the 1972 election would therefore have to be extremely speculative, the results would appear to confirm the judgment that the Democratic coalition formed at the 1932 realignment has become extremely unstable.

Fig. 4.—Election group scores on realignment
and normal competition

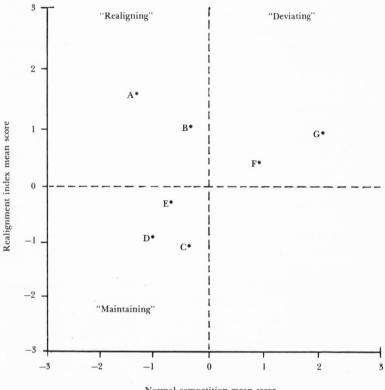

Normal competition mean score

left, or maintaining, quadrant, as the result of their negative re-alignment and negative normal competition mean scores. Groups F and G are placed in the upper right, or deviating, quadrant, by sharing slightly positive realignment index mean scores and positive normal competition scores. No groups fell into the lower right quadrant which would be characterized as elections in which there was competition without any elements of realignment, a condition which is probably rarely, if ever, fulfilled.

While the categorizations of the seven election types into three broader categories on the basis of the relationships shown in Figure 4 are based on only three of the six identified differentiating characteristics, they are themselves held to be useful heuristic constructs developed from the three most important differentiating dimensions.

The heuristic value of the broader categorizations is shown in Table 4 in which the election types and categories developed in this chapter are compared with those developed by Pomper and Burnham. In terms of definition of electoral realignments, Table 4 shows three general areas of agreement and two of disagreement among the methods employed here (hereafter referred to as the "Shade" types and categories) and those of Burnham and Pomper. All three studies agree that a realignment occurred during the period surrounding the Civil War, although Burnham identifies 1854 as the peak of the realigning period, the Shade typology identifies the 1860 presidential election, and Pomper the 1864 election. The disagreement between the Shade and Pomper findings may merely be a matter of rhetoric, for the Shade typology recognizes that the realignment initiated in 1860 was not stabilized until 1864, so the Shade and Pomper typologies can be said to be in general agreement on the definition of this realignment.

A second general area of agreement occurs in 1896, defined by Shade as realigning and by Burnham as the election immediately following the midpoint of his realigning period. Pomper, however, classifies 1896 as a noncritical realignment, and he is somewhat at odds with the conclusions of Shade and Burnham. The final area of agreement centers around the election of 1932, identified by both Shade and Pomper as realigning, and by Burnham as the election immediately following the peak of a realignment period. Pomper, however, also classifies the election of 1928 as realigning, while Shade types the election as a nonrealigning conversion of the previous Republican coalition. Pomper's classification of 1928 as realigning does, however, bracket Burnham's 1930 midpoint of his realigning period.

The two general areas of disagreement occur around the 1876 election when the coalition of Lincoln Republicans established in the 1860s began to break down. Burnham classifies 1874 as the midpoint of another period of realignment; Pomper classifies the elections of 1872 and 1876 as maintaining the Lincoln coalition. The sharp disagreement between the conclusions of Pomper and Burnham can perhaps be best understood in terms of the more detailed Shade typology, in which 1876 is a disintegrative election with the previously dominant Republican coalition beginning to

TABLE 4.—COMPARISON OF ELECTORAL TYPOLOGIES

| Election | Shade (type) | Shade (category) | Pomper[a] (type) | Burnham[b] (Period midpoint) |
|---|---|---|---|---|
| 1860 | *Multiparty realignment* | *Realigning* | Deviating | *Realignment period,* midpoint, 1854 |
| 1864 | Restabilizing | Maintaining | *Realigning* | |
| 1868 | Reconstituting | Maintaining | Maintaining | *Realignment period,* midpoint, 1874 |
| 1872 | Reconstituting | Maintaining | Maintaining | |
| 1876 | Disintegrative | Deviating | Maintaining | |
| 1880 | Deviating | Deviating | Deviating | |
| 1884 | Deviating | Deviating | Maintaining | |
| 1888 | Deviating | Deviating | Deviating | *Realignment period,* midpoint, 1894 |
| 1892 | Deviating | Deviating | Converting | |
| 1896 | *Two-party realignment* | *Realigning* | Maintaining | |
| 1900 | Converting | Maintaining | Maintaining | |
| 1904 | Converting | Maintaining | Maintaining | |
| 1908 | Converting | Maintaining | Deviating | |
| 1912 | *Multiparty realignment* | *Realigning* | Deviating | |
| 1916 | Restabilizing | Maintaining | Maintaining | |
| 1920 | *Two-party realignment* | *Realigning* | Maintaining | |
| 1924 | Converting | Maintaining | *Realigning* | |
| 1928 | Converting | Maintaining | *Realigning* | *Realignment period,* midpoint, 1930 |
| 1932 | *Two-party realignment* | *Realigning* | Maintaining | |
| 1936 | Reconstituting | Maintaining | Maintaining | |
| 1940 | Reconstituting | Maintaining | Maintaining | |
| 1944 | Reconstituting | Maintaining | Maintaining | |
| 1948 | Disintegrative | Deviating | Maintaining | |
| 1952 | Deviating | Deviating | Deviating | |
| 1956 | Reconstituting | Maintaining | Deviating | |
| 1960 | Deviating | Deviating | Converting | |
| 1964 | Reconstituting | Maintaining | Converting | |
| 1968 | Disintegrative | Deviating | Deviating[c] | |

a. Pomper, *Elections in America,* p. 111.
b. Burnham, *Critical Elections,* p. 16.
c. ... according to Pomper's criteria; see *Elections in America,* p. 104

break down, but with the Democrats unable to establish an en-during coalition to replace it. This is evident in the long series of deviating elections shown by Pomper and Shade in the period between 1880 and the 1896 realignment. This period of what might be termed electoral chaos seems analagous to the chaotic situation described by Kuhn as occurring when a scientific paradigm breaks down but is not immediately replaced by a new one: "Because it demands large-scale paradigm destruction and major shifts in the problems and techniques of normal science, the emergence of new theories is generally preceded by a period of pronounced professional insecurity. As one might expect, that insecurity is generated by the persistent failure of the puzzles of normal science to come out as they should. Failure of existing rules is the prelude to a search for new ones" (pp. 67–68). Hence, Burnham's technique of identifying shifts in electoral cleavage may have caused him to make a mistake: the insecurity of the electorate, suggested by a series of deviating elections, and the failure of the Democrats to develop a paradigm to replace the decomposed Lincoln nationalism did not indicate a period of genuine realignment. This explanation demonstrates the value of the distinctions made in the fully developed Shade typology, in particular the distinction between disintegrative and realigning elections.

One final point of disagreement among the typologies concerns the Shade definition of the elections of 1912 and 1920 as realigning. Burnham gives no indication of realignment during this period, and Pomper classifies the 1912 election as deviating and the 1920 election as maintaining, purely on the basis of the conception of the Republican Party as the majority party after what he calls the noncritical conversion of 1896. The electoral upheaval of 1912 brought on by the Progressives was surely as convulsive as the multiparty factionalism of 1860, and seems more clearly to belong in a classification with that election than with the elections of 1952 and 1956, as in the Pomper typology. While Pomper also classified 1860 as deviating, the Shade typology presents a more realistic conception of electoral alignments by categorizing 1860 and 1912 as unique upheavals of the electorate, both of which were restabilized in the following election with the return of the incumbent to power and a decline of third party movements. This phenomenon clearly indicates an ability of the major parties to adapt to issues generated from outside their normal structures, and this characteristic of these elections clearly deserves to be distinguished from the relatively mild ideological conflict that characterized the elections of 1952 and 1956. The inductive Shade typology enables one to make this differentiation undoubtedly because of the broader base of electoral characteristics from which it was derived, as opposed to the Pomper typology which was based on only two characteristics of elections.

The inductive typology of elections developed in this chapter has been shown to be in general congruence with previously developed typologies; in cases of incongruence, it was argued to have greater explanatory ability of the incongruent phenomena than either of the two previously developed typologies. While the three broad categories developed by analysis of the three greatest differentiating dimensions were shown to be heuristically useful in comparison with the Pomper and Burnham typologies, the more detailed typology developed on the the basis of the additional information contained in the remaining three dimensions will be used in later analyses.

# 5. Social Change and Election Types

To IDENTIFY patterns of societal change that coincide with the patterns of electoral alignment given in chapter 4, I will use a stepwise multiple discriminant analysis of the groupings of elections based upon the 54 measures of societal change described in Table 5. The specific variables in the table have been classified as to the general type of societal change that they are intended to measure.

The first 15 variables are measures of general social change and are for the most part self-explanatory. In general, they measure only the change in the phenomenon that has taken place since the previous election. In some cases, for example, marriage and suicide rates, the level of the variable was also included, as observation of the raw data indicated that in these cases levels as well as rates of change could discriminate election types. The social variables selected were intended to measure the degree of conflict or harmony among individual members of society. The measurement of postage stamp issuance was intended to measure expansion or contraction of channels of communication among individuals. The measurement intended by the other variables is generally self-evident.

The measures of political change describe several phenomena. Variables 17 and 18 measure the amount of intraparty competition for the presidential nomination. Variables 19–21 measure the issue-distances of the major party platforms; 22–24 indicate variance in the campaign efforts of the major parties, measured in dollar terms. Variables 25–29 measure different dimensions of the relationship of the incumbent president with the legislatures seated during his administration. The twenty-ninth measures the "efficiency" of these legislatures by calculating the percentage of bills introduced that actually passed both houses. Finally, variable

TABLE 5.—INDEPENDENT VARIABLES IN DISCRIMINANT ANALYSIS[a]

I. Measures of Social Change
   1. change in population
   *2. change in urbanization
   *3. change in birth rate
   4. marriage rate
   *5. change in marriage rate
   *6. change in divorce rate
   7. change in death rate
   8. suicide rate
   *9. change in suicide rate
   *10. change in mental hospital admission rate
   11. internal migration rate
   12. change in internal migration rate
   13. number of immigrants admitted
   14. change in number of immigrants admitted
   15. change in religious membership
   16. change in per capita postage stamps issued

II. Measures of Political Change
   17. # convention ballots required to nominate winner
   18. # convention ballots required to nominate loser
   *19. per cent bipartisan platform pledges
   20. per cent contradictory platform pledges
   *21. per cent unique platform pledges
   22. per cent difference in campaign spending (winner/loser)
   *23. change in winner's campaign spending
   24. change in loser's campaign spending
   25. congressional houses controlled by incumbent party—1st Congress
   *26. congressional houses controlled by incumbent party—2d Congress
   27. number of vetoes by incumbent
   28. number of incumbent's vetoes overridden
   29. congressional efficiency
   *30. presidential incumbent running for reelection

III. Measures of Public Policy Change
   *31. change in federal nondefense expenditures
   32. change in federal defense expenditures
   *33. change in per capital federal taxation
   34. change in per pupil education expenditures
   35. change in active duty military personnel

IV. Measures of Economic Change
   36. change in per capita GNP
   *37. change in industrial production index
   38. change in wholesale price index
   39. change in consumer price index
   40. change in average industrial wage index
   *41. change in gross farm income
   *42. change in total business concerns
   43. business failure rate
   *44. change in business failure rate
   45. short term interest rate
   46. change in short term interest rate
   *47. long term interest rate
   *48. change in long term interest rate

TABLE 5—*Continued*

V.  Measures of Intellectual Change
   *49. change in per capita newspaper circulation
    50. change in book and pamphlet copyright registrations
    51. change in periodical copyright registration
VI.  Measures of Technological Change
   *52. change in patent applications
    53. change in mineral energy fuel consumption
    54. change in pig iron production

---

a. An asterisk preceding a variable number indicates that the variable was selected for inclusion in the discriminant function. Data sources for the variables
listed in this table are detailed in Appendix 2.

30 measures the impact of the advantage of the incumbent president in seeking re-election.

Five measures of public policy change were included: 31–33
measure policy changes at the federal level; 34 shows policy change
at the state and local levels, in terms of expenditures for education; 35 indicates increases in military personnel and hence measures the tendency of an administration to resort to force in conduct
of foreign affairs.

Thirteen measures of economic change were developed, each
self-explanatory. Intellectual change was operationalized by variables measuring newspaper circulation and book, pamphlet, and
periodical copyright registrations. Technological change was shown
by measures of change in patent applications, mineral energy fuel
consumption, and pig iron production.

The 21 variables identified by an asterisk in the table were those
selected for inclusion in the discriminant function because they
contribute to the discrimination of the election types. The re-
mainder did not contribute to the discrimination. Surprisingly,
each area of societal change contributed at least one variable to
the discriminant function. Since the original data were standardized prior to calculation of the discriminant coefficients, the relative importance of each variable in showing election types can be
seen by examining the size of that variable's coefficient in the discriminant function.[1] These coefficients are shown in Table 6.

The discriminant coefficients clearly indicate that the electorate
is most responsive to change in the economic system. The variable

1. Morrison, *Multivariate Statistical Methods*, p. 130.

TABLE 6.—DISCRIMINANT FUNCTION COEFFICIENTS

| Independent Variables | Discriminant Coefficient |
|---|---|
| Social conflict | |
| change in urbanization | −.09 |
| change in birth rate | .24 |
| change in marriage rate | .38 |
| change in divorce rate | −.14 |
| change in suicide rate | .30 |
| change in mental hospital admissions | −.05 |
| Political conflict | |
| per cent bipartisan platform pledges | .17 |
| per cent unique platform pledges | .11 |
| change in winner's campaign expenditures | −.19 |
| houses of 2d Congress controlled by incumbent party | .09 |
| presidential incumbent running for reelection | .20 |
| Public policy | |
| change in federal nondefense expenditures | .69 |
| change in per capita federal taxation | −.72 |
| Economic change | |
| change in industrial production | 1.00 |
| change in gross farm income | .23 |
| change in total business concerns | .23 |
| change in business failure rate | .34 |
| long term interest rate | .35 |
| change in long term interest rate | −.32 |
| Intellectual change | |
| change in per capita newspaper circulation | −.18 |
| Technological change | |
| change in patent applications | .07 |

with the greatest discriminating power is the one that measures change in industrial production. While other economic variables included in the function have smaller coefficients, all point to a conception of a prosperous economy. Long-term interest rates are high and stable, and while the business failure rate has increased, it has been accompanied by an increase in the total number of concerns in business, suggesting that a prosperous economy may encourage an increase in speculative, and hence more risky, business activity. Prosperity in the industrial sector of the economy is matched, albeit to a somewhat lesser degree, by an increase in gross farm income.

A second area of change to which the electorate appears highly responsive is the public policy output of the incumbent administration. The discriminant function suggests that the electorate responds sharply to change in per capita federal taxation, as well as to change in federal nondefense, or domestic, spending.

The coefficients of the social change variables indicate a trend of what might be termed social harmony. Birth and marriage rates increase; divorce, urban migration, and mental hospital admission rates decline. The increase in suicide rate may be an anomaly, but perhaps may result from the greater psychological pressure of individual failure in a period of overall harmony and prosperity.

The coefficients of the political change variables confirm the long-acknowledged advantage of the presidential incumbent, although it is interesting to note that the size of the discriminant coefficients indicates that this advantage is less important than the policy outputs of the previous administration in determining the type of electoral alignment most likely to follow. The importance of presidential campaigns is reflected in the coefficients of the variables describing the amount of agreement in the content of the platforms of the major parties and by the decline in monetary effort expended in the campaign by the winning party. In general, the campaign described in the discriminant function is one in which an incumbent candidate, with majority support in the Congress immediately preceding the election, runs on a platform that is either in agreement with or talks past the opposing party, and spends less effort campaigning than in the previous election. This appears to be a neat summary of what has been called normal politics. The lack of conflict in party platforms suggests that ideological conflict was held to a minimum, another characteristic of normal politics.

In the last two areas of societal change analyzed, the discriminant function indicates a decline in per capita newspaper circulation, suggesting a decline in electoral attentiveness during periods of normal politics, and an increase in patent applications, suggesting increased technological creativity in periods of prosperity and social harmony.

The general situation following from the discriminant analysis is that of normal politics in a economically prosperous and socially harmonious period. The relationships of the individual election types to these phenomena can be analyzed by computation of discriminant scores for each election on the discriminant function.[2]

2. Discriminant scores are computed by substituting the original standardized score for each variable into the discriminant function, multiplying by the discriminant coefficient, summing, and adding the constant term for each

These scores are shown in Table 7, which shows that reconstituting elections score highest on the discriminant function, indicating that elections which strengthen support for existing political coalitions are generally accompanied by periods of greatest prosperity and harmony, and are periods of normal politics. Disintegrative elections score second highest, indicating that the ideological deviance of the third party movements initiated in those elections was not accompanied by any societal crisis of the magnitude required to effect a shift in paradigms. Converting elections also score positively, but far lower on the scale than reconstituting elections, suggesting that the concurrent differences in scale of prosperity and harmony may be responsible for the moderate shifting of voters that distinguishes converting from reconstituting elections.

Four types of elections scored negatively: two-party realignments, multiparty realignments, deviating, and restabilizing elections. The negative scores of these elections indicate that substantial voting shifts are generally accompanied by economic decline, social disharmony, and ideological conflict in periods of abnormal politics.

Multiparty realignments and restabilizing elections score very closely on the scale. The proximity of these scores and the fact that the elections that comprise these types are contiguous in time lends further support to the suggestion made earlier that the realignments of 1860 and 1912 spread out over two elections. Deviating elections bear higher negative scores than both multiparty realignments and restabilizing elections, calling attention to the need for additional research on what distinguishes a deviating election from a realignment. The answer may lie in the responses of the parties to the societal crisis at hand. As suggested earlier, the period 1880–96 was ripe for the establishment of a realignment behind the Democratic Party, as the Republican coalition had begun to disintegrate as early as 1876. Instead, the period was marked by a series of deviating elections, accompanied by persistent cycles of economic instability and social conflict. The suggestion made here is that the failure of the Democratic Party to institutionalize a

---

group provided by the discriminant analysis. For a more complete description of this procedure see Francis J. Kelly, Donald L. Beggs, and Keith A. McNeil, *Research Design in the Behavioral Sciences: Multiple Regression Approach* (Carbondale: Southern Illinois University Press, 1969), pp. 234–39.

TABLE 7.—DISCRIMINANT SCORES BY ELECTION GROUP

| | |
|---|---|
| **Realigning elections** | |
| A. Two-party | |
| 1896 | −733.5 |
| 1920 | −733.5 |
| 1932 | −733.5 |
| B. Multiparty | |
| 1860 | −107.8 |
| 1912 | −107.8 |
| | |
| **Maintaining elections** | |
| C. Reconstituting | |
| 1868 | 629.1 |
| 1872 | 629.1 |
| 1936 | 629.3 |
| 1940 | 629.0 |
| 1944 | 629.1 |
| 1956 | 629.1 |
| 1964 | 629.1 |
| D. Restabilizing | |
| 1864 | −130.0 |
| 1916 | −130.0 |
| E. Converting | |
| 1900 | 43.1 |
| 1904 | 43.1 |
| 1908 | 43.1 |
| 1924 | 43.1 |
| 1928 | 43.1 |
| | |
| **Deviating elections** | |
| F. Deviating | |
| 1880 | −378.4 |
| 1884 | −378.4 |
| 1888 | −378.4 |
| 1892 | −378.4 |
| 1952 | −378.4 |
| 1960 | −378.4 |
| G. Disintegrative | |
| 1876 | 113.9 |
| 1948 | 111.2 |
| 1968 | 113.1 |

political paradigm to replace Lincolnian nationalism was the major stumbling block to a stable realignment in the period beginning in 1880. Hence, the ideological bases of party behavior may well be the distinguishing feature of deviating versus realigning elections.

Finally, the most negative scores on the scale belong to two-party realignments. This confirms Burnham's conclusion that realignments generally occur in periods of social unrest, economic decline, and ideological conflict. Thus two-party realignments must come closest to fulfilling the definition of paradigm shifts presented in chapter 2. This point will be examined in chapter 6.

In summary, the multiple discriminant analysis showed that reconstituting, converting, and disintegrative elections were generally associated with periods of social and economic prosperity, and realigning, deviating, and restabilizing elections were associated with periods of opposite characteristics.

# 6. An Assessment of the Theory of Political Paradigms

Results of the empirical tests from chapters 4 and 5 will now be re-examined to determine the amount of support they provide for the hypotheses stated at the conclusion of chapter 3. There are some methodological caveats that must be considered in interpretation of these results, and I will attempt a general assessment of the theory of political paradigms and an analysis of the implications of the theory for the future of American politics.

### Empirical Support for Hypotheses

At the conclusion of chapter 3, five hypotheses derived from the theory of political paradigms were developed which, if confirmed by empirical investigation, would support the validity of the theory.

The first hypothesized relationship was that an inductive comparison of the historical distributions of the electorate would distinguish paradigm-shifting elections from normal competition elections. Support for this hypothesis was provided in two ways. Two of the six differentiating dimensions identified in the alpha factor analysis clearly described phenomena associated with sharp and durable shifts of electoral loyalty, a condition that constitutes one of the characteristics of paradigm shifts. A general category of realigning elections, consisting of two inductively derived types, was identified in analysis of the results of a hierarchical cluster analysis of the scores of the individual elections on each of the six differentiating dimensions. The analyses suggest that the elections of 1860, 1896, 1912, 1920, and 1932 are distinguishable in that they comprised sharp and durable shifts of the electorate. Hence, the inductive analyses of electoral distributions tend to confirm the existence of the first relationship hypothesized from the theory of political paradigms.

The second hypothesis was that paradigm-shifting elections would coincide with some type of societal crisis in order to inspire the attentiveness of the electorate, as suggested by the quotation from Burke in chapter 2. The phenomena described by the discriminant function provided a scale of societal harmony/disharmony, and the discriminant scores of the elections identified as realigning were toward the negative, or crisis, end of the scale. These scores indicate, then, that realigning shifts of the electorate did in fact coincide with periods of individual social conflict, economic decline, increased intellectual attentiveness, and an abnormal increase in the issue-distances or ideologies of the major parties. The fact that restabilizing and deviating elections also scored negatively on the discriminant phenomenon indicates that not all societal crises cause realignments and suggests that some unique response to the crisis, perhaps by the parties, is required to effect a shift in the content of the governing paradigm.

This suggestion leads directly to consideration of the third hypothesis, that at points of paradigm shifts political parties would serve the purpose of institutionalizing competitive paradigms. Indeed the shifts in party loyalties were said to be an intrinsic component of the exemplary past achievement aspect of paradigm shifts. Analysis of support for this hypothesis must be derived from an analysis of the ideological positions of the parties in the elections classified as realigning.

The election of 1860 clearly presented an ideological choice to the electorate. Historian Elting Morison points out that four distinct ideological positions were represented by the four competing parties. The three Democratic splinter parties all harkened back to the existing Jacksonian paradigm of political laissez-faire.[1] Bell held for absolute laissez-faire, or business as usual; Douglas attempted a compromise solution within the paradigm; and Breckenridge felt that the breakdown of the Jacksonian paradigm over the slavery issue should lead to a division of paradigms within the political community, with separate paradigms for homogeneous

1. For an interpretation of the content of this paradigm, see Alan P. Grimes, *American Political Thought* (New York: Holt, Rinehart and Winston, 1966), pp. 184–87.

subgroups.[2] Lincoln alone offered a new paradigm based upon the ideological premise that nationalism superseded the benefits of political laissez-faire, and that the nation-state should be preserved at all costs. While it may have taken two presidential elections and a civil war to completely effect the shift from the Jackson to the Lincoln paradigm, the ability of the paradigm to attract the loyalty of the political community (of the North) to go to war to defend it should in no way detract from the conception of the dominance of the paradigm. Rather it should point to the strength of the paradigm content, as contemporary politicians are finding that support for paradigms does not always include a mandate to commit the community to the use of force on its behalf. The sharpness of the split at the election of 1860 and the enduring dominance of the Republican Party in the series of elections that followed until 1876 demonstrates that the election of 1860 fulfilled the conditions of a paradigm shift, thus supporting the third hypothesis.

In the next election defined as realigning, that of 1896, the electorate faced a dichotomous but ideologically distinct choice. In this realignment the electorate forsook the rising populism of the free-silver Democrats in favor of the conservative protectionism of the McKinley Republicans. That the election was dominated by economic issues is a clear reflection of the economic decline of the 1890s under less radical, but still Democratic, leadership. In fact, the ideological break between Bryan and the leadership provided by Cleveland indicated a complete breakdown of the preceding paradigm as both parties offered alternatives ideologically distinct from the content of the previously governing paradigm. (As it has been previously suggested that after the disintegration of the Lincoln coalition in 1876 no truly dominant paradigm emerged until 1896, it would probably be more accurate to state that in 1896 both parties offered paradigms to fill an ideological void rather than to replace a previously dominant paradigm.)

According to the typology, the next realignment occurred in 1912 when, after a period of conservative Republican protectionism, the electorate was faced with another multiparty choice. In a drastic shift from Taft conservatism, the electorate aligned behind

2. For a more complete discussion of the issue-distances between the candidates mentioned, see Elting Morison, "The Election of 1860," in *History of American Presidential Elections, 1789–1968*, ed. Arthur M. Schlesinger (New York: McGraw-Hill, 1971), 2:1097–1122.

the New Freedom liberalism of Wilson, although it took the re-stabilizing election of 1916 to effect the shift in paradigm. The New Freedom paradigm had an uncharacteristically brief period of dominance; its liberal promise became entangled in the First World War, and, in 1920, another realignment was effected when a disenchanted electorate endorsed Harding's proposed return to neo-isolationism and economic individualism over Cox's effort to maintain the New Freedom paradigm by endorsing its content as well as Wilson's internationalism. Hence, the period 1912–20 was characterized by rapid shifts of electoral loyalty between two competing paradigms: economic individualism and neo-isolationism, and New Freedom liberalism and internationalism.

The economic individualist paradigm dominated the administrations of Harding, Coolidge, and Hoover, through the social crisis produced by the Great Depression. At the election of 1932, Roosevelt's proposed New Deal paradigm of positive governmental economic action replaced the conservative paradigms espoused by Hoover, and a paradigm shift was effected that some analysts, as well as the electoral typology, suggest remains dominant in the current American political community.[3]

This brief examination of the ideological distances of the parties at the elections defined as realigning generally confirms Burnham's conclusion that realignments are accompanied by greater than normal ideological conflict, thus supporting the validity of the third hypothesis derived from the theory of political paradigms.

There is little empirical support for the last two hypotheses developed in chapter 3, that periods prior to paradigm shifts would be marked by distortions of normal competition and that periods following such shifts would be marked by restoration of normal competition. There seems to be no unique pattern of electoral distributions that can be expected to precede or follow paradigm shifts. In fact, one striking feature of the realigning elections identified in the typology is their lack of periodicity, a characteristic suggested by Burnham and others as distinctive of electoral realignments. The periods between paradigm shifts suggested in the typology are thirty-six years, sixteen years, eight years, and twelve years, with the current paradigm suggested as entering its

3. For example see Lowi, *The End of Liberalism*; he argues that the paradigm was in the process of final breakdown in the late 1960s.

fortieth year. This finding is in direct conflict with Burnham's argument that realignments occur once a generation, or once every thirty to thirty-eight years, but it supports Pomper's contention that there is no theoretical justification for a cyclical conception of realignments.[4]

In summary, the empirical analyses provide substantial support for the validity of the theory of political paradigms in conjunction with three of the five hypotheses derived from the original statement of the theory. The lack of support for two hypotheses may suggest that political scientists have been negligent in attempting to uncover the characteristics of normal politics in American political history.

## METHODOLOGICAL CAVEATS

While this discussion indicated general support for the validity of the theory of political paradigms, the results of the analyses conducted to "test" the hypotheses are subject to some methodological caveats of interpretation. The hypotheses were not tested in any strict statistical, probabilistic sense, but rather were argued to be congruent with the findings of inductive analyses of the dependence structure of multivariate data observations. Strictly speaking, no statistical inference can be made to the probability that the "confirmed" hypotheses were not falsely accepted.

In addition, although standard data sources were employed,[5] the data in the discriminant analysis must be considered "soft" for the period preceding 1900, particularly for the era of the Civil War.

Finally, there is an implicit flirtation with the so-called ecological fallacy, which points out that relationships based on aggregate data are not necessarily good substitutes for relationships based on individual data. While this analysis has focused on the aggregate behavior of the political community in periods of paradigm shifts, the implicit assumption has been that support for these aspects of the theory of political paradigms implies support for the individual

4. Arguments for the periodicity of realignments are contained in Burnham, *Critical Elections*, and Sellers, *Equilibrium Cycle*; arguments opposing the necessary periodicity appear in Pomper, *Elections in America*, and "Classification of Presidential Elections."

5. See Table 2 for data sources on election characteristics and Appendix 2 for data sources on phenomena of societal change.

social psychological aspects of the theory. While it is agreed that survey data would provide a more accurate representation of individual behavior, the absence of any such data for the period prior to 1936 precludes its use in the analysis of paradigm shifts as the typology indicates that the last such shift occurred in 1932. Therefore, rather than fall prey to the "academic overkill" that Price argued followed the original statement of the ecological fallacy by W. S. Robinson,[6] the possibility of such a fallacy is noted, but it is argued that the strength of the deductive theoretical relationship shown between aggregate behavior and individual behavior in the development of the theory suggests that the ecological fallacy has been avoided in this research. Final resolution of this question will lie with a later generation of political scientists with more extensive survey data archives and perhaps additional electoral realignments to subject to analysis.

Despite these caveats, my main conclusion is that American political history since 1860 is best described as a sequence of shifting ideological paradigms which define the rules of the game, to use Schattschneider's phrase. If the analogy of scientific paradigms can be extended further, the criterion of successful science developed by James B. Conant, a tutor of Kuhn's at Harvard, can be applied to the political system. Conant argued that science is successful not to the extent that it approaches truth, but only to the extent that it maintains its continuity.[7] By this criterion the American political system can be described as highly successful as it approaches its two-hundredth birthday. But it may be best to end on a note of caution by observing that the historical ability of the system to adapt to social, economic, political, intellectual, and technological changes provides no guarantee that the process is automatic, and care must be taken to insure that this ability will be preserved.

6. Price, "Micro- and Macro-Politics," and Robinson, "Ecological Correlations and the Behavior of Individuals," *American Sociological Review* 15 (1950) : 351–57.

7. *Science and Common Sense* (New Haven: Yale University Press, 1951).

# Appendix 1. Methodology

AN EXAMINATION of the underlying mathematical principles of factor analysis will be followed by a discussion of the use of alpha factor analysis.[1]

## FACTOR ANALYSIS

Factor analysis is an applied form of what mathematicians refer to as the "characteristic value" problem. This problem is one of describing the numerical relationships among large sets of numbers, in matrix form, in a more concise manner than the original matrix itself.

Consider a square matrix of numbers, A, where:

$$A = \begin{bmatrix} a11 & a12 & \ldots\ldots\ldots\ldots\ldots & a1_n \\ a21 & a22 & \ldots\ldots\ldots\ldots\ldots & a2_n \\ {}' & {}' & & {}' \\ {}' & & & {}' \\ {}' & & & {}' \\ an_1 & an_2 & \ldots\ldots\ldots\ldots\ldots & ann \end{bmatrix}$$

The characteristic value problem is that of finding n scalar parameters, $\lambda$, (single numbers), which satisfy the equality

$$A\underline{x} = \lambda\underline{x},$$

where $\underline{x}$ are identical n-element vectors. If such scalars can be determined, they could then be said to be "equivalent" to the origi-

1. The discussion of factor analysis that follows is intended to be as untechnical as possible, but thorough in its coverage. For a still less technical description of the technique, see Nie, Bent, and Hull, *SPSS*, pp. 208–26. For a more detailed, but highly technical discussion, see Morrison, *Multivariate Statistical Methods*, pp. 221–93.

nal matrix A. One obvious solution is $x = 0$, but this is dismissed as trivial since the $\lambda$s could then take on any value. The restraint $\underline{x} \neq 0$ is then placed upon the solution, and the above equality is rewritten

$$A\underline{x} = \lambda I\underline{x},$$

where I is simply an identity matrix. By simple algebraic manipulation this can be rewritten

$$(A - \lambda I)\underline{x} = 0.$$

Since it has already been determined that if $\underline{x} = 0$, the solution would be trivial, then a nontrivial solution exists if and only if

$$/ \, A - \lambda I \, / = 0,$$

which is generally referred to as the "characteristic equation" of the original matrix, A.[2]

Algebraic theory has determined that the characteristic equation of an n-by-n element matrix has n roots, or values of $\lambda$. These roots, $\lambda$, are variously referred to as the characteristic roots, latent roots, or eigenvalues of the original matrix of observations. Hence, by solution of the characteristic value problem, the numerical relationships contained in the original n-by-n matrix can be represented in abbreviated form by the n scalars (single numbers), $\lambda$. Each $\lambda$ also has an associated vector $\underline{x}$, generally referred to as its eigenvector, which enables it to fulfill the originally stated equality

$$A\underline{x} = \lambda \underline{x}.$$

In the statistical technique of factor analysis, the matrix that is solved for its characteristic roots is a correlation matrix. Two generic types of factor analysis have been developed: principal components analysis and factor analysis proper. In the first case, the correlation matrix is unaltered and merely subjected to a characteristic value solution. It can be shown statistically that the sum of the characteristic values of a correlation matrix equals the total variance of the matrix, which is in turn given by the sum of the elements down the diagonal of the matrix.[3] Since characteristic roots generally differ widely in numerical magnitude, the value of

---

2. The term included in the slashes, / . . . /, is intended to mean "the determinant of" rather than "the absolute value of."
3. For proof of this statement see Morrison, pp. 222–29.

each root is often used to determine how much of the original variance is associated with the eigenvector of that characteristic root. Quite often almost the entire amount of variance in the correlation matrix is associated with a much smaller number of eigenvectors, and hence principal components analysis is often employed as a data reduction technique, with the smaller number of eigenvectors used to replace the larger number of original variables contained in the correlation matrix.[4]

Factor analysis proper, like principal components analysis, also has the property of data reducibility. However, in factor analysis proper the object is to separate (or factor) the original variance in the correlation matrix into two parts: variance that is shared by the variables in the matrix and variance that is unique to any single variable. This is accomplished by altering the correlation matrix prior to extracting the characteristic roots. The alteration generally involves substituting the squared multiple correlations of each variable with the others into the diagonal elements of the matrix, i.e., in place of the "perfect" 1.00 correlations of each variable with itself. The sum of these squared multiple correlations, now the diagonal elements, is then used as an estimate of the shared or common variance of the original correlation matrix.[5] The matrix altered by insertion of the squared multiple correlations is referred to as the "reduced correlation matrix," and in factor analysis proper this is the matrix that is subjected to a characteristic value solution.

4. This should not imply that data reduction is the only application of principal components analysis. In a general sense it can be used to test hypotheses about the dependence structure of multivariate observations. In the paper by Weber, "Dimensions of State Party Systems," principal components analysis was used to test the hypothesis that the construct of party competition at the state level was composed of a single dimension. A principal components analysis of a larger number of variables that purported to measure state party competition identified four eigenvectors that were associated with large enough amounts of the original variance that Weber concluded that they measured separate dimensions of the construct.

5. While early factor analysis programs considered the sum of the squared multiple correlations as an adequate estimate of shared variance (see "BMDO3M: General Factor Analysis," in Dixon, *BMD: Biomedical Computer Programs*), more recent programs incorporate iterative procedures to estimate variable "communalities," which are then summed and employed as an estimate of shared variance. See "BMDX72: Factor Analysis," in W. J. Dixon, ed., *BMD: Biomedical Computer Programs X-series Supplement* (Berkeley: University of California Press, 1970), and Nie, Bent, and Hull. Additional methods of communality estimation are discussed in these references.

Once the characteristic roots and eigenvectors of a correlation or reduced correlation matrix are determined, the eigenvectors are usually subjected to additional linear transformations in order to improve the interpretability of the phenomena which they describe. A standard transformation is to calculate "factor loadings" for each eigenvector. This is accomplished by multiplying each element of the eigenvector by the square root of its associated eigenvalue. The factor loading estimated by this computation is then interpreted as the correlation coefficient, or loading, of each original variable with each eigenvector, or factor.[6] A matrix of factor loadings then displays the correlational relationships between the original variables and the reduced number of factors, thus facilitating the interpretation of the phenomena described in the factors.

The pattern of correlational relationships displayed in any single factor loading matrix is not unique, however, and by subjecting the factor loading matrix to additional linear transformations an infinite number of factor loading matrices can be developed from the original characteristic vectors and eigenvectors. The purpose of these transformations is generally to relocate the axes of the factors in n-dimensional space in order to maximize some previously determined criterion of interpretability. Hence the analyst must predetermine a criterion for deciding which factor loading matrix to employ as the most appropriate description of the original variables for the purposes of his analysis. This problem will be discussed in the next section.

To summarize the basic characteristics of factor analysis, it has been shown capable of examining the numerical relationships of a relatively large number of original variables, of distinguishing the common or shared relationships among these variables (if desired), and of representing these relationships in a smaller number of eigenvectors or factors. By application of linear transformations to the eigenvectors, the phenomena described in these reduced number of factors can be subjected to theoretical interpretation. These are the basic characteristics of any factor analysis. In recent years, however, additional capabilities have been developed for specific factor analysis applications, and we will now discuss the factor analysis model to be employed here.

6. The validity of this statement is demonstrated in Morrison, p. 226.

## ALPHA FACTOR ANALYSIS

In the preceding discussion, the problem of selecting the "most appropriate" factor loading matrix to represent the original variables was left unsolved. The most common solution to this problem is to "rotate" the factor loading matrix through the space containing the infinite number of solutions until one fulfilling a set of criteria designated as "simple structure" has been found.[7] The criteria for determining simple structure have been arbitrarily defined by L. L. Thurstone:

1. Each row of the matrix should contain at least one zero.
2. Each column of the matrix should contain at least as many zeroes as there are factors.
3. Every pair of columns should contain several variables whose loadings vanish in one column but not in the other.
4. If there are four or more factors, every pair of columns should contain a large number of variables with zero loadings in both columns.
5. Conversely, for every pair of columns only a small number of variables should have nonzero loadings in both columns.[8]

While these criteria are undoubtedly the most popular in contemporary factor analysis applications, other decision criteria have been developed. The criterion employed in this study is to select the factor loading matrix that maximizes Cronbach's coefficient of generalizability. This attempt to introduce elements of statistical inference into a factor analytic solution was developed by Henry F. Kaiser and John Caffrey and termed "alpha factor analysis" after the coefficient employed.[9]

Broadly stated, the goal of alpha factor analysis is to generalize from some (usually nonrandom) sample of variables that purport to measure a phenomenological construct to the universe of content of that construct, based upon information contained in a population of cases. Note that this goal is quite different from the usual concept of statistical inference, which is to generalize to some

7. While the word rotate was employed to maintain the heuristic geometrical analogy, selection of simple structure matrices is generally determined by one of several alternative mathematical solutions which are discussed in Nie, Bent, and Hull.
8. Morrison, pp. 278–79.
9. "Alpha Factor Analysis," *Psychometrika* 30 (1965): 1–14.

population of individuals from a sample of cases on certain specific variables. To distinguish these types of inference, the type employed in alpha factor analysis is sometimes referred to as "psychometric inference," after the journal *Psychometrika*, in which the techniques of this type of inference were generally first published.

The rationale behind the concept of psychometric inference has developed slowly over half a century. Its roots lie in the original concepts of reliability theory which attempted to determine the confidence that psychologists could have in the reliability of tests developed to measure some specific nonphysical phenomena. In the classical period of reliability theory, which traces back at least to Spearman in 1904,[10] reliability was defined as the correlation between "equivalent" measures of a phenomenon. These coefficients were generally calculated by dividing test responses into halves, and calculating the correlation, or "split-half" coefficient. High coefficients were then taken to indicate that the test provided a relatively true measure of the phenomenon. Many criticisms of the split-half approach were formulated, the most telling of which being the arbitrary nature in which the test scores were generally divided in half.

In 1951, Lee J. Cronbach derived his "alpha coefficient of reliability" which was shown to be the mean of all possible split-half coefficients resulting from different splittings of a test.[11] He concluded, "[The alpha coefficient] is therefore an estimate of the correlation between random samples of items from a universe of items like those in the test" (p. 297).

In a landmark article that literally revolutionized the field of reliability theory, Robert C. Tryon pointed out that reliability coefficients like Cronbach's alpha had greater conceptual validity than the generally narrow theorems of reliability theory, which had not been revised since Spearman. Tryon developed the broader concept of "behavior domain validity," and argued, "A statistic that is more meaningful than the reliability coefficient is the correlation of $X_t$ [observed variables] with a score on the domain of components comparable to $X_t$. A domain score of an individual

10. "The Proof and Measurement of Association between Two Things," *American Journal of Psychology* 15 (1904):72–101.
11. "Coefficient Alpha and the Internal Structure of Tests," *Psychometrika* 16 (1951):297–334.

would be the best criterion of his status in the property X, as operationally defined."[12] He then derived the "behavior domain validity coefficient" of a variable which estimates how close observed scores on a variable are to "their ranking in a perfectly reliable measure of the property X, as operationally defined." The behavior domain validity coefficient was shown to be simply the square root of the reliability coefficient, and was defined as "The correlation between a sample [measure] and its perfect criterion measure of the property X, as operationally defined" (p. 237). Hence to test the domain validity of a measurement device, the coefficient is calculated, and if it is too low it is concluded that the device selected to measure the phenomenon under investigation must be improved.

In 1963, Cronbach and his associates extended further Tryon's concept of behavior domain validity to a more formal theory of generalizability,[13] and it was upon this development that Kaiser and Caffrey developed the application of the renamed "alpha coefficient of generalizability" to the factor analysis model.

The basis of alpha factor analysis has been clearly stated by Kaiser and Caffrey: "The principle upon which the present method of factor analysis is based is that common factors are to be determined which have maximum correlation with corresponding universe common factors. This compelling psychometric concept of assessing the confidence one may have in a variable, here a common factor, by determining the correlation of its representation for the variables to be observed with its 'true' representation for all variables in the universe is due to Tryon, as his notion of 'behavior domain, i.e., universe, validity' " (p. 5). Hence alpha factor analysis, in addition to sharing the properties of data reducibility and determination of shared relationships, incorporates the property of selection of a factor loading matrix that is most generalizable to the universe of content of the phenomenological construct under investigation by maximizing Cronbach's alpha and concurrently Tryon's behavior domain validity coefficient.

12. "Reliability and Behavior Domain Validity," pp. 236–37.
13. Cronbach, Nageswari Rajaratnam, and Goldine C. Gleser, "Theory of Generalizability: A Liberalization of Reliability Theory," *British Journal of Statistical Psychology* 16 (1963):137–63.

# Appendix 2. Data Sources for Independent Variables Listed in Table 5

1. U.S. Department of Commerce, Bureau of the Census, *Historical Statistics of the United States, Colonial Times to 1957* (Washington: Government Printing Office, 1960), Series A1–A2;

 ———, *Historical Statistics of the United States, Colonial Times to 1957; Continuation to 1962 and Revisions* (Washington: Government Printing Office, 1965), Series A1–A2. (Hereafter, these two sources will be referred to as *Historical Statistics.*)

 ———, *Statistical Abstract of the United States, 1970* (Washington: Government Printing Office, 1971), Table 2. (Hereafter this source will be referred to as *Statistical Abstract.*)

2. *Historical Statistics,* Series A195, A20; *Statistical Abstract,* Table 14.

3. *Historical Statistics,* Series B20; *Statistical Abstract,* Table 53.

4. *Historical Statistics,* Series D764, D770; *Statistical Abstract,* Table 53.

5. Ibid.

6. *Historical Statistics,* Series D772; *Statistical Abstract,* Table 53.

7. *Historical Statistics,* Series B155, B129 (prior to 1900 the death rate is for the State of Massachusetts only); *Statistical Abstract,* Table 53.

8. Data for 1860–96 were obtained from A. D. Frenay, *The Suicide Problem in the United States* (Boston: Badger, 1927); data for later years were obtained from *Historical Statistics,* Series B128, and *Statistical Abstract,* Table 73.

9. Ibid.

10. *Historical Statistics,* Series B273, B274; *Statistical Abstract,* Table 100.

11. *Historical Statistics,* Series C5, C7; *Statistical Abstract,* Table 37.

12. Ibid.

13. *Historical Statistics,* Series C88; *Statistical Abstract,* Table 128.

14. Ibid.

15. *Historical Statistics,* Series H539, H541, H543; *Statistical Abstract,* Table 50 (data are for Presbyterian, Methodist, and Southern Baptist sects only).

16. *Historical Statistics,* Series R142; *Statistical Abstract,* Table 743.

17. Richard C. Bain, *Convention Decisions and Voting Records* (Washington: Brookings, 1960), and Schlesinger, ed., *History of American Presidential Elections.*

18. Ibid.

19–
21. These three variables measure the amount of congruence or incongruence between the two major party platforms. They were originally developed by Gerald Pomper and are more fully described in *Elections in America.* The content analysis technique employed in the derivation of these variables is described in an appendix to that work. The original platforms themselves are contained in Schlesinger.

22. Schlesinger.

23. Ibid.

24. Ibid.

25. *Historical Statistics,* Series Y139, Y142; *Statistical Abstract,* Table 543.

26. Ibid.

27. U.S. Congress, *Presidential Vetoes* (Washington: Government Printing Office, 1961), and *Statistical Abstract,* Table 545. (Vetoes by lame duck incumbents and vetoes of bills for the relief of specific individuals were excluded from the analysis.)

28. Ibid.

29. *Historical Statistics,* Series Y129, Y132; *Statistical Abstract,* Table 544.

30. Schlesinger.

31. *Historical Statistics,* Series Y355; *Statistical Abstract,* Table 562.

32. *Historical Statistics,* Series Y351–Y353; *Statistical Abstract,* Table 562.

33. *Historical Statistics,* Series Y264; *Statistical Abstract,* Table 564.

34. U.S. Department of Commerce, Bureau of the Census, *Long Term Economic Growth* (Washington: Government Printing Office, 1966), Series B43 (hereafter this source will be referred to as *Economic Growth*); *Statistical Abstract,* Table 170.

35. *Historical Statistics,* Series Y763; *Statistical Abstract,* Table 384.

36. *Historical Statistics,* Series F4, F16; *Statistical Abstract,* Table 470.

37. *Economic Growth,* Series A15–A16; *Statistical Abstract,* Table 1113.

38. *Historical Statistics,* Series E1, E13, E25; *Statistical Abstract,* Table 517.

39. *Historical Statistics,* Series E113, E148; *Statistical Abstract,* Table 523.

40. *Historical Statistics,* Series D574, D604, D696; *Statistical Abstract,* Table 344.

41. *Historical Statistics,* Series K125, K139; *Statistical Abstract,* Table 929.

42. *Historical Statistics,* Series V1; *Statistical Abstract,* Table 740.

43. *Historical Statistics,* Series V2; *Statistical Abstract,* Table 740.

44. Ibid.

45. *Economic Growth,* Series B81; *Statistical Abstract,* Table 677.

46. Ibid.

47. *Economic Growth,* Series B74–B75; *Statistical Abstract,* Table 1100.

48. Ibid.

49. *Historical Statistics,* Series R170, R176; *Statistical Abstract,* Table 765.

50. *Historical Statistics,* Series W52–W53; *Statistical Abstract,* Table 772.

51. *Historical Statistics,* Series W57; *Statistical Abstract,* Table 772.
52. *Historical Statistics,* Series W66; *Statistical Abstract,* Table 814.
53. *Historical Statistics,* Series M78; *Statistical Abstract,* Table 1022.
54. *Historical Statistics,* Series M207; *Statistical Abstract,* Table 1054.

# UNIVERSITY OF FLORIDA MONOGRAPHS

## Social Sciences